LUCENT LIBRARY OF
BLACK HISTORY

AFRICAN AMERICAN
LITERATURE
Sharing Powerful Stories

By Meghan Sharif

Portions of this book originally appeared in
African American Literature by Stephen Currie.

LUCENT
P R E S S

Published in 2018 by
Lucent Press, an Imprint of Greenhaven Publishing, LLC
353 3rd Avenue
Suite 255
New York, NY 10010

Designer: Deanna Paternostro
Editor: Siyavush Saidian

Library of Congress Cataloging-in-Publication Data

Names: Sharif, Meghan.
Title: African American literature: sharing powerful stories / Meghan Sharif.
Description: New York : Lucent Press, 2018. | Series: Lucent library of black history | Includes index.
Identifiers: ISBN 9781534560772 (library bound) | ISBN 9781534560789 (ebook)
Subjects: LCSH: African Americans–History–Juvenile literature. | American literature–African American authors–History and criticism–Juvenile literature. | African Americans in literature–Juvenile literature.
Classification: LCC E185.S53 2018 | DDC 810.9'9287–dc23

Printed in the United States of America

CPSIA compliance information: Batch #BS17KL: For further information contact Greenhaven Publishing LLC, New York, New York at 1-844-317-7404.

Please visit our website, www.greenhavenpublishing.com. For a free color catalog of all our high-quality books, call toll free 1-844-317-7404 or fax 1-844-317-7405.

CONTENTS

Foreword 4

Setting the Scene: A Timeline 6

Introduction:

African American Literature: An Overview 8

Chapter One:

Stories Spoken and Sung: 1600–1800 10

Chapter Two:

Stories of Slavery: 1800–1865 24

Chapter Three:

Postbellum Stories: 1865–1918 42

Chapter Four:

New York City Stories: 1918–1940 56

Chapter Five:

Civil Rights Stories: 1940–1969 70

Chapter Six:

Today's Stories: 1970–Present 85

Notes 98

For More Information 104

Index 107

Picture Credits 111

About the Author 112

FOREWORD

Black men and women in the United States have become successful in every field, but they have faced incredible challenges while striving for that success. They have overcome racial barriers, violent prejudice, and hostility on every side, all while continuing to advance technology, literature, the arts, and much more.

From medicine and law to sports and literature, African Americans have come to excel in every industry. However, the story of African Americans has often been one of prejudice and persecution. More than 300 years ago, Africans were taken in chains from their home and enslaved to work for the earliest American settlers. They suffered for more than two centuries under the brutal oppression of their owners, until the outbreak of the American Civil War in 1861. After the dust settled four years later and thousands of Americans—both black and white—had died in combat, slavery in the United States had been legally abolished. By the turn of the 20th century, with the help of the 13th, 14th, and 15th Amendments to the U.S. Constitution, African American men had finally won significant battles for the basic rights of citizenship. Then, with the passage of the groundbreaking Civil Rights Act of 1964, many people of all races began to believe that America was finally ready to start moving toward a more equal future.

These triumphs of human equality were achieved with help from brave social activists such as Frederick Douglass, Martin Luther King Jr., and Maya Angelou. They all experienced racial prejudice in their lifetimes and fought by writing, speaking, and peacefully acting against it. By exposing the suffering of the black community, they brought the United States together to try and remedy centuries' worth of wrongdoing. Today, it is important to learn about the history of African Americans and their experiences in modern America in order to work toward healing the divide that still exists in the United States. This series aims to give readers a deeper appreciation for and understanding of a part of the American story that is often left untold.

Even before the legal emancipation of slaves, black culture was thriving despite many attempts to suppress it. From the 1600s to 1800s, slaves developed their own cultural perspective. From music, to language, to art, slaves began cultivating an identity that was completely unique. Soon after these slaves were granted citizenship and were integrated into American society, African American culture burst into the mainstream. New generations of authors, scholars, painters, and singers were born, and they spread an appreciation for black culture across America and the entire world. Studying the contributions of these talented individuals fosters a sense of optimism. Despite the cruel treatment and racist attitudes they faced, these men and women never gave up, changing the world with their determination and unique voice. Discovering the triumphs and tragedies of the oppressed allows readers to gain a clearer picture of American history and American cultural identity.

Here to help young readers with this discovery, this series offers a glimpse into the lives and accomplishments of some of the most important and influential African Americans across historical time periods. Titles examine primary source documents and quotes from contemporary thinkers and observers to provide a full and nuanced learning experience for readers. With thoroughly researched text, unique sidebars, and a carefully selected bibliography for further research, this series is an invaluable resource for young scholars. Moreover, it does not shy away from reconciling the brutality of the past with a sense of hopefulness for the future. This series provides critical tools for understanding more about how black history is a vital part of American history.

SETTING THE SCENE:

1667
The first of the Slave Codes, laws that made it illegal to teach slaves how to write, are passed.

1923
The first issue of *Opportunity: Journal of Negro Life* is published by Charles S. Johnson.

1845
Frederick Douglass publishes *Narrative of the Life of Frederick Douglass, an American Slave*, one of the most famous slave narratives of all time.

| 1667 | 1773 | 1845 | 1902 | 1923 |

1773
Phillis Wheatley publishes a book of poetry, becoming the first black author in North America to ever publish a book.

1902
Langston Hughes, a poet, novelist, and playwright, is born.

A TIMELINE

1969
Maya Angelou's *I Know Why the Caged Bird Sings* is published to great critical acclaim.

2015
Ta-Nehisi Coates publishes *Between the World and Me*, which wins the National Book Award for Nonfiction and highlights black struggles in 21st century America.

| 1969 | 1993 | 2006 | 2015 | 2016 |

2006
Octavia E. Butler, one of the most respected voices in science fiction and fantasy writing, passes away.

1993
Toni Morrison becomes the first African American to win the Nobel Prize in Literature.

2016
Colson Whitehead receives the Pulitzer Prize and the National Book Award for his *The Underground Railroad*; *Hidden Figures*, a nonfiction account of black female NASA scientists in the 1960s, is published and adapted into a highly successful film.

INTRODUCTION

AFRICAN AMERICAN LITERATURE: AN OVERVIEW

The very first Africans to arrive in the New World brought with them a rich tradition of story, song, and folklore. Although nearly all black people living in America in the early years were brought against their will as part of the slave trade, they did not allow the institution of slavery to silence their voices. Throughout the years, African Americans contributed their unique perspectives to the landscape of American literature. Despite prejudice, lack of respect, legal challenges, and barriers to education, black writers persevered and created lasting works that endure to this day.

The earliest African literary talents in North America were part of what was known as an oral tradition—the literature of this time was spoken or sung rather than written down. Many of the slaves who were brought across the ocean from Africa were forced to learn English on their own, with no access to education or instruction. In fact, many slaves who lived together in the same household may not have spoken the same language, as their countries of origin may have been far apart. This meant they had only English to communicate with each other. Despite the barriers, these displaced men and women continued to share these stories and folklore with each other and pass them from one generation to the next. Many of these folktales would come to influence authors in future generations.

Not Afraid to Fight

Very few black people in the early days of North American history were able to read or write, but a few black men and women did write and publish work as early as the 18th century. Later, as the abolitionist movement began to take shape, the voices of African American authors became crucial in calling for an end to slavery for good. Escaped slaves wrote alarming accounts of their experiences in slavery, and these dramatic narratives became extremely popular. Their autobiographical accounts had great influence in swaying public opinion against slavery and were an important part of the politics of the day.

After the American Civil War and the legal end of slavery in America, black writers turned from exposing the evils of slavery to exposing the evils of racial inequality that still existed throughout the country. Even though slavery was at an end, autobiographical accounts of life in the South after the war still cried out against unfair treatment. Nonfiction writing was still the largest part of African American literature, and it eventually expanded to include political pamphlets and speeches.

The Harlem Renaissance and the civil rights movement brought black voices in front of even broader audiences. The Harlem Renaissance brought artistic, creative writing by African American authors to the forefront. More and more people began to read these diverse stories about the experience of being black in America. The civil rights movement called for even more political writing, and African American authors answered that call. Speeches, essays, and fiction that highlighted experiences of racism and inequality were an important part in the fight for equal rights for African Americans.

Today, African American literature encompasses all types and genres of writing. Black authors of the 20th and 21st centuries have won countless literary awards and prizes, published successful bestselling novels, and gained recognition as talented lyricists and poets. To this day, African American authors draw inspiration from the work of the earliest black writers. The long history of African American literature will no doubt form a foundation for many great literary works that will be published in the years to come.

CHAPTER ONE

STORIES SPOKEN AND SUNG: 1600–1800

In America in 1600, the vast majority of the black population was made up of men and women forced to labor as slaves. By 1860, there were about 4 million slaves living in the United States. While not all Americans of African descent were kept as slaves, slaves accounted for about 89 percent of the black population in America at this time. The abuses of slavery were numerous: grueling work for no pay and minimal food and shelter; laws that allowed slave owners to beat their slaves and treat them terribly with few consequences; and the trauma of people being ripped from their cultures and homes to find themselves in a strange new land. Families were broken apart, and many of the slaves working together under a particular slave owner had come from different places and spoke different languages.

Even free black Americans faced a great deal of discrimination. While they could legally work and were not owned by anyone, their lives were far from easy. Most lived in poverty, and they were prevented from holding certain jobs or living in certain communities based on the color of their skin. They had limited access to education, and most could not read or write. Furthermore, they were undoubtedly affected by the universal racism of American society at the time.

Given these extraordinarily difficult circumstances, one would not expect there to be much African American literature in this time period. With very little or no education, constant and exhausting work, and rigid boundaries surrounding every aspect of their lives, African Americans would have had little time or opportunity to be creative. Nevertheless, black people living in these challenging times continued to tell stories. There were laws that made it illegal to teach slaves to write, but those same slaves crafted and passed down stories by word of mouth and in song. Despite the fact that those brought over against their will from Africa learned English as a second language, they took the language and made it their own as they retold and shared folktales with one another. These early examples of African American literature were passed down from one generation to the next.

In years to come, these earliest literary efforts of African Americans would inform future generations of black writers. The voices of these early writers would be passed down, despite attempts to silence them. Over time, African American literature would become more and more mainstream and reach more and more people. African American authors of the 21st century stand on the foundation built by those brave men and women of the 1600s and 1700s who told their stories and began a rich literary tradition that still resounds today.

Through the Spoken Word

Nearly all the African slaves in the Americas came from societies that had no formal system of reading and writing. The lack of a written language did not imply, however, that these societies lacked literature. On the contrary, West African cultures had a rich and vibrant tradition of stories, poems, and songs. They spread these works through the spoken word, by means of storytellers and singers, rather than through written texts. Historians and other experts describe this way of passing stories from one generation to the next as an oral tradition.

The first Africans in the New World brought their oral traditions with them. The stories they told were the stories popular among the West African groups they belonged to. Their poetry had been created by previous generations over the course of many years. These stories and songs offered hope and comfort to the newcomers. Though they had been taken from their homes and families, they could at least remember the literary traditions of their homeland. Indeed, the early slaves told these stories and sang these songs frequently. As one historian wrote, "The elements of storytelling were included in the only 'baggage' [the slaves] could carry with them: their traditional styles [and] their ways of performing

BANNEKER'S LETTER

Benjamin Banneker was a free black man who lived most of his life in Maryland. Fascinated by science, mathematics, and engineering, Banneker built what may have been the first clock produced in the United States. He also helped plan the layout of Washington, D.C., and wrote almanacs detailing his knowledge of astronomy.

In 1791, Banneker wrote a famous letter to Thomas Jefferson, who was then serving as George Washington's secretary of state. Like most white

Benjamin Banneker was a scientist and inventor who was the author of almanacs that described facts about the natural world.

and celebrating."[1]

Over time, the connections between black Americans and their African origins began to fade. Christianity slowly started to replace African religions; English soon replaced African languages. The songs and stories of West Africa were living traditions, however, interpreted in different ways by different storytellers and singers, and as the lives of the new African Americans changed, their oral literature changed alongside it. By the early 1800s, the folklore of black Americans remained related to the traditions of West Africa, but it had become something new: a body of literary work uniquely rooted in the black American experience.

Americans of his time, Jefferson believed that black people were much less intelligent than white people. Banneker's letter sought to prove Jefferson wrong. He argued that blacks and whites were much more alike than they were different. "One universal Father hath given being to us all," Banneker wrote. "However variable we may be in science or religion, however diversified in [social class] or color, we are all in the same family."[1] The lowly position of blacks in America, Banneker asserted, had nothing to do with their natural ability and everything to do with racism and slavery.

In case Jefferson did not find this argument compelling, Banneker also enclosed one of his almanacs. He hoped that upon seeing the book, Jefferson would be impressed with Banneker's insight and intelligence and would rethink his position. Jefferson was interested in Banneker's almanac and persuasive argument. Banneker's letter is remembered today less for the influence it had on Jefferson's politics than for the clear thinking it demonstrated on the subject of race.

1. Quoted in Louis Haber, *Black Pioneers of Science and Invention*. Orlando, FL: Harcourt, Inc., 1970, p. 9.

Folktales

The stories of early African Americans took a variety of forms. Some of the best known today are a series of animal folktales that focus on a character called Br'er (sometimes written as Brer) Rabbit. These tales were collected by a white author—Joel Chandler Harris—based on his interviews with southern slaves. Br'er Rabbit is a trickster—a sly creature who relies on his wits to escape his more powerful enemy, Br'er Fox. Though other characters are included in the dozens of Br'er Rabbit tales recorded by 19th century folklorists, Br'er Rabbit is the hero of most of these stories. The central theme of many of them is Br'er

The character of Br'er Rabbit used his wits to escape difficult situations.

Rabbit's ability to outsmart the fox.

In one famous story, for instance, Br'er Fox has captured the little rabbit and is wondering how best to torment him. Br'er Rabbit, seemingly alarmed, begs his enemy not to throw him into a nearby tangle of weeds and thorns. "I don't keer [care] w'at [what] you do wid [with] me, brer Fox … so [long as] you don't fling me in dat [that] brier-patch," pleads the rabbit, "Roas' me, Brer Fox … but don't fling me in dat brier-patch."[2] Convinced that Br'er Rabbit's distress is genuine, Br'er Fox promptly tosses his enemy into the thorny bush. He regrets it, though, when he hears the rabbit scampering happily away. Br'er Rabbit tricked the fox because he knew he could escape if he was thrown into the briars.

Another series of stories told by African Americans before the Civil War involves a fictional slave, typically named John. Most of these stories describe John's attempts to fool his master or to gain his freedom. In one story, for example, John claims to be in direct contact with God. He arranges for a friend to climb to the top of a tree, carrying a variety of items with him. While his master watches, John then calls for the items one by one. The master is shocked to see each item fall from the tree. Believing that John really is giving orders to God, the foolish master sets John free and gives him his own land and a large sum of money.

These stories, like most other black folktales, powerfully reflect the realities of life in slavery. The John tales, for instance, sprang directly from the experiences of slaves with harsh masters. Similarly, slaves often identified with Br'er Rabbit, who has physical disadvantages but often prevails against Br'er Fox. The rabbit's victories over his enemy gave the slaves hope that they too might overcome their own disadvantages. Though the slave owners were richer, better educated, and better armed than the slaves, the Br'er Rabbit stories inspired slaves to think that their masters were not necessarily more intelligent—and might not always come out on top.

Spirituals and Work Songs

Song lyrics represented another important part of the West African oral tradition. As with stories, the songs of 19th century African Americans were not the same as those of West Africans of older generations. The realities of the black experience in America led to songs with very different themes and topics from the songs native to West Africa. Just as the stories of the black oral tradition formed part of the foundation for African American literature, so too did the songs.

Many of the earliest songs sung by African Americans were work songs. It was common for black laborers to sing as they performed their jobs, especially when groups of workers were carrying out a repetitive task, such as harvesting crops or pounding in fence posts. Some songs were funny and light-hearted. One line from a song titled "Charleston Gals" was,

> I kep' a walking and they kep'
>   a talking,
> I danced with a gal with a
>   hole in her stocking.[3]

By far the best-known African American folk songs of the time, though, are religious songs called spirituals. The spirituals, which date to the mid-1700s or earlier, expressed the adopted Christian faith of African American slaves. Some of the spirituals were joyous, celebrating the expected triumph of Jesus over evil and waiting for the day when the singer would be taken up to heaven. "O, blow your trumpet, Gabriel," was a line from a song of this type, referencing a Christian belief that the angel Gabriel would announce the end of the world with a blast of a trumpet:

> Blow your trumpet louder;
> And I want dat trumpet to
>   blow me home
> To my new Jerusalem.[4]

Though the Christian message of salvation was a powerful one for black Americans, not all spirituals were joyful. On the contrary, many were introspective, sometimes even sad. These were known as sorrow songs. Meant to be sung slowly and softly, sorrow songs mourned the trials of life on Earth and called on God and Jesus for emotional support. These songs were popular among slaves as well, particularly after a difficult day of work.

A third type of spiritual retold stories from the Bible. Most related stories from the Old Testament, such as the narrative of Adam and Eve or the visions of the prophet Ezekiel. The tale of the Exodus was a particularly common subject for spirituals. This story tells how Moses led the Hebrew people out of slavery in Egypt toward the promised land. For the black people of the American South, the similarities between the Hebrews and their own lives were obvious. The chorus to one famous spiritual about the Exodus is:

Go down, Moses, way down in Egypt's land,
Tell old Pharaoh, Let My people go.[5]

Similar to the stories and the work songs of the African American oral tradition, spirituals were among the first examples of black literature in the United States. Even today, they remain among the best known of all art forms created by black Americans. They are widely admired for their imagery and their ability to touch listeners and readers hundreds of years after their creation. The themes and ideas in the words of spirituals continue to influence current African American literature.

The Written Word

The bulk of early African American literature was spoken or sung, not written, and given the low levels of literacy among blacks of the time, this is not surprising. Nevertheless, a few black writers of the late 1700s and early 1800s did manage to get their work published. The first was a man named Jupiter Hammon. Born in New York in 1711, Hammon lived his whole life as a slave. His owners, however, allowed him considerable independence from an early age. Unlike almost all other slaves of the 1700s, for instance, Hammon went to school and learned to read and write. Later, he became a preacher who spoke often to slave congregations; he may even have kept the accounts for his owners' businesses.

In addition to these talents, Hammon was also a poet. In 1761, he became the first African American to publish a piece of writing—a long religious poem titled "An Evening Thought. Salvation by Christ with Penitential Cries." The verses reflected Hammon's deep faith and his certainty that Jesus will offer salvation to all Christians. "Salvation comes by Jesus Christ alone," Hammon wrote at the start of his poem,

The only Son of God;
Redemption now to every one
That love his holy Word.[6]

Over the next few decades, Hammon published several more

AN

ADDRESS

TO THE

NEGROES

IN THE

STATE OF NEW-YORK.

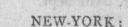

BY JUPITER HAMMON,

Servant of JOHN LLOYD, jun. Esq. of the Manor of Queen's Village,
Long-Island.

" Of a truth I perceive that God is no respecter of
" persons:

" But in every Nation, he that feareth him and work-
" eth righteousness, is accepted with him."——

Acts x. 34, 35.

NEW-YORK:

Published by SAMUEL WOOD, No. 362 Pearl-street.

1806.

Shown here is a later edition of one of the best-known works of writing by Jupiter Hammon: a speech he gave in 1786.

works, including both poetry and prose. Hammon's best-known piece of writing today is a speech he gave in 1786, which he published in pamphlet form a year later. The speech is titled "Address to the Negroes in the State of New York." In this speech, Hammon urged his younger black listeners to put Christianity at the center of their lives. "Those of you who can read," he told his audience, "I must beg you to read the Bible … What shall I say to them who cannot read? … I beg of you to spare no pains in trying to learn to read."[7]

In his speech, however, Hammon did not focus entirely on religion. He also wrote of slavery and what it meant to be a slave. Living as he did—in a world made by and for white people—Hammon was cautious in his statements about slavery. He claimed that he had no desire for freedom and stressed the responsibilities of being a slave. Still, he left no doubt that he disapproved of slavery. "I should be glad," he asserted, "if others, especially the young Negroes, were to be free."[8]

Wheatley's Poetry

Though Hammon was the first African American to publish his writing, he was not the best-known black writer of his time. That honor goes to a poet named Phillis Wheatley. Born in about 1753 in West Africa, Wheatley was brought to Massachusetts as a girl and sold into slavery. She quickly learned English and impressed her owners with her intelligence and curiosity. They soon taught her to read and write and raised her to be a Christian with an understanding of the Bible.

Wheatley began writing poetry as an adolescent. When she was still a teenager, she published her first poem, "On the Death of Rev. Mr. George Whitefield," and followed it with other works in the next several years. Though Wheatley's writing style has gone out of favor since her time, it was very much in line with the literary trends of the era. Her poems were marked by metaphors, classical references, and formal, complex language. A patriotic poem she wrote dating from 1776, for instance, begins with the line "Celestial choir, enthroned in realms of light."[9]

The themes of Wheatley's poems were typical of her era, too. Poets of the period often wrote about abstract topics, for example, and Wheatley followed the trend. She entitled one poem "On Virtue," and her work included verses about ideals such as wisdom, devotion, and education. As with her writing style,

Phillis Wheatley was one of the first African American poets.

E   M   S

O N

OUS SUBJECTS,

GIOUS AND MORAL.

B Y

LIS WHEATLEY,

VANT to Mr. JOHN WHEATLEY,
OSTON, in NEW ENGLAND.

O   N   D   O   N:

BELL, Bookseller, Aldgate; and sold by
nd BERRY, King-Street, BOSTON.

M DCC LXXIII.

Wheatley's themes are no longer common topics among the general public. The combination can make it difficult for modern readers to appreciate Wheatley's work; the editors of one anthology of black literature noted that her poetry comes across today as "pious sentimentalizing about Truth, Salvation, Mercy, and Goodness."[10]

Still, though literary tastes have changed, Wheatley's poetry was quite popular in her time. George Washington read and enjoyed at least one of her works, and a book of her poems sold well in both England and the colonies. It surely helped Wheatley's reputation that her choice of topics was mainstream and inoffensive. Her poems rarely mentioned slavery or race, which allowed white people to enjoy her work without having to confront difficult moral and political issues. In fact, one of the few poems that discusses Wheatley's race actually describes her gratitude at being removed from Africa:

'Twas mercy brought me from
    my Pagan land,
Taught my benighted soul
    to understand
That there's a God, that there's
    a Saviour too:
Once I redemption neither
    sought nor knew.[11]

ON TRIAL FOR POETRY

Phillis Wheatley was able to overcome many barriers in her quest to become a published poet. Her race, however, was certainly a handicap. Some publishers refused to print her book because she was black. Other whites insisted that people of African descent were unable to write poetry at all, let alone construct the sophisticated stanzas Wheatley produced. In 1772, in fact, a committee of Bostonian scholars met to determine whether Wheatley was really the author of the poems she had published. The committee eventually ruled that the poems were indeed hers, but the fact that the question came up at all indicates the willingness of 18th-century white Americans to doubt the intelligence and achievements of black people.

Though Wheatley was released from slavery as a young woman, she did not have much opportunity to enjoy her freedom. Her later life was marked by tragedy. She married, but she and her husband had difficulty finding work and lived in poverty for most of their marriage. She had three children, none of whom survived infancy. Wheatley's health was never good, and in 1784, she died, probably not much older than 30.

Another Early Poet

Hammon and Wheatley were the best-known black writers of their time, but they were not the only ones. According to many sources, for instance, a Massachusetts woman named Lucy Terry Prince composed a poem titled "Bars Fight" in 1746. The poem describes a surprise attack by Native Americans on a Massachusetts settlement known as "the Bars," leading to the deaths of several settlers. The poem consists of rhyming couplets that detail the grim fates of the colonists:

Oliver Amsden, he was slain,
Which caused his friends much
grief and pain.[12]

Historians still debate how much of "Bars Fight," was truly original to Prince. She never published the poem and may never have written it down. For many decades, the poem circulated only as part of the settlers' oral traditions. Even if Prince wrote a poem about the fight, the transcription may not represent her original work. Nonetheless, there is some evidence that Prince did compose a poem about the fight, and as a result, several historians credit her as being among the first African American poets.

From a stylistic point of view, the works of Hammon, Prince, and other early black writers may not have been innovative. Their insights were not always compelling or unique. As 20th century black writer and critic Arna Bontemps wrote, these earliest writers were followed "by writers who had more to say and said it more effectively."[13] Nonetheless, when their work is viewed alongside the rich oral tradition that developed among black Americans in the 1700s and beyond, it is clear that these early writers laid the groundwork for future black authors. The writers who came later owe much to the imagery of the early spirituals, the biting humor of the Br'er Rabbit stories, and the courage and talent of the authors and poets who came before them.

CHAPTER TWO

STORIES OF SLAVERY: 1800–1865

Although northern states had begun to move away from the institution of slavery by the early 1800s, the cruel and unjust practice was far from over. The economy of the American South had only grown more dependent on slave labor to produce huge profits on cotton plantations. More and more black Americans were living their lives as slaves under harsh conditions, with little access to education. The idea of ending slavery as the North had done was hugely unpopular with white southerners, and influential politicians, scientists, and religious leaders of the day made many arguments in favor of slavery. In fact, in order to justify the oppression of African Americans slaves, anti-abolitionists wrote many religious and political pamphlets and speeches claiming that slavery was not only good, but also necessary.

Black writers of the 1800s raised their collective voice in opposition to these pro-slavery arguments. African Americans living as free men and women in the North wrote and published well-argued treatises against slavery that countered those of southern political leaders. They took their arguments apart point by point and explained how abolition was the morally correct choice. Other authors, who had experienced the brutality of slavery themselves, wrote accounts of their lives and personal experiences to show how unjust the system was. Many of these works still resonate today.

Walker and Garnet

One of the first black writers to attack slavery was a man named David Walker, born in North Carolina in 1796. In 1829, soon after moving to

Writing such as this poster helped spread the message of the abolitionist movement.

Boston, he published *Appeal to the Colored Citizens of the World*. Better known today as Walker's *Appeal*, the book was a bitter argument against slavery. Because Walker had been free from birth, he had never experienced slavery directly; nonetheless, Walker had spent much of his life in the South. As a result, his understanding of slavery was genuine—and thorough. "I do not speak from hear say," Walker assured his readers. "What I have written, is what I have seen and heard myself. No man may think that my book is made up."[14]

What set Walker's *Appeal* apart from other antislavery writings was not so much Walker's knowledge of slavery, however. It was his passion. The book is filled with emotional appeals for blacks of all backgrounds to join together in condemning slavery—and ending it. Walker made liberal use of italics and exclamation marks in his book to emphasize his statements. He frequently inserted multiple exclamation points at the end of his sentences as a display of passion. "I tell you Americans!" he warned, "that unless you speedily alter your course [by abolishing slavery], *you* and your *Country are gone*!!!!!!"[15]

Minister and author Henry Highland Garnet was another black man who wrote frequently about abolition. Unlike Walker, Garnet spent his first years as a slave. Born in 1815 in Maryland, he escaped from slavery with his family at the age of nine with the help of the Underground Railroad. Garnet's best-known writing was a speech he gave in 1843, which became known as his "Call to Rebellion." In this fiery piece of writing, Garnet advocated the use of violence to overturn the slave system. Using language and emotional appeals that would have pleased even the most extreme abolitionists, Garnet laid down a challenge to the slaves of the South. "IT IS YOUR SOLEMN AND IMPERATIVE DUTY," he insisted, "TO USE EVERY MEANS, BOTH MORAL, INTELLECTUAL, AND PHYSICAL THAT PROMISES SUCCESS."[16]

More Authors Against Slavery

Black women writers served the cause of abolition as well. Frances Ellen Watkins Harper, born in Baltimore, Maryland, in 1825, was one example. Among the best-known African American writers of the period, Harper published dozens of poems and several prose works. Many date from the years after the Civil War, but some of her most famous works were written while slavery was still very much alive.

Frances Harper wrote a famous poem about the challenging experience of motherhood as a slave.

A DIFFICULT TALE

Moses Roper was born into slavery around 1815. Mistreated by a succession of masters, Roper made several unsuccessful attempts to escape to the North. In 1833, however, his master went bankrupt and he signed on as a deckhand on a ship headed to New York. He eventually went to England and wrote a book about his life titled *A Narrative of the Adventures and Escape of Moses Roper, from American Slavery*, which was published in 1838. This was among the earliest and most popular slave narratives to be

Moses Roper's memoir includes detailed accounts of the abuses he suffered as a slave.

One of Harper's best known poems, titled "The Slave Mother," was written in 1854. It describes the feelings of a slave woman about to be separated from her son. It began,

> *Heard you that shriek? It rose*
> *So wildly on the air,*
> *It seem'd as if a burden'd heart*
> *Was breaking in despair.*[17]

Another notable antislavery writer of the period was a man named Martin Delany. Delany was born in Virginia in 1812 and, like Walker and Harper, was never a slave. A man of many talents, Delany worked at various times as a newspaper editor, a doctor, a soldier, and a politician. Unlike many other black people of the time, Delany doubted that published. The following excerpt describes one of his earliest attempts to run to freedom:

> I then came to a rail fence, which I found it very difficult to get over, but breaking several rails away, I [succeeded]. They then called upon me to stop, more than three times, and I not doing so, they fired after me, but the pistol [did not fire]. This is according to law; after three calls they may shoot a runaway slave. Soon after the one on the horse came up with me, and catching hold of the bridle of my horse, pushed the pistol to my side; the other soon came up, and breaking [off] several stout branches from the trees, they gave me about a hundred blows. They did this very near to a planter's house; the gentleman was not at home, but his wife came out, and begged them not to kill me so near the house: they took no notice of this, but kept on beating me.[1]

1. Moses Roper, *A Narrative of the Adventures and Escape of Moses Roper, from American Slavery*. Philadelphia, PA: Merrihew & Gunn, 1838. HTML e-book, accessed May 18, 2017. docsouth.unc.edu/fpn/roper/roper.html.

abolition would raise African Americans to a position of equality with white Americans. In accord with this belief, Delany published a book in 1852, in which he encouraged black people to leave the United States altogether to return to their home countries in Africa.

Delany's wish was for African Americans to completely remove themselves from the direct influence of whites. Out of the range of whites, he argued, blacks could establish their own governments and revive their own traditions. "Every people should be the originators of their own designs," he wrote, "the projector of their own schemes, and the creators of the events that lead to their destiny."[18] Delany was not the only thinker of his time who saw mass emigration as the solution to the problem of race in America. Several white writers and politicians of the time offered similar proposals. Logistically, however, it was not possible to send all American blacks elsewhere, and Delany's wish never became reality.

Personal Stories

The majority of abolitionist writers—both white and black—of the early 1800s had spent most or all of their lives in freedom. That was not the case, however, for the authors of another form of antislavery literature: slave narratives. Slave narratives could be book-length volumes or short pamphlets. In either case, they were sold to the public as genuine accounts of slave life, written or told by a former slave who had either purchased their freedom or escaped to the free North. The best of these books were strong statements against the slave system, but they were also uplifting stories that showcased the strength, courage, and resilience of men and women who had once been held in bondage. The slave narrative was an important expression of African American literature in the years before the American Civil War.

Not every slave narrative was the absolute truth, however. As northern opinion swung more and more strongly against slavery in the 1840s and 1850s, some publishers began issuing narratives that were far more fiction than fact. Though the title pages of these works carried the names of former slaves, the real authors were professional writers who paid little attention to the slaves' actual experiences. Publishers knew their audiences, and they were aware that a narrative full of danger and drama would sell, regardless of its authenticity, while a narrative that lacked these features would not. Given the intense competition among publishers of the time to find an audience for their books, it is not surprising that some sacrificed the truth in favor of profits.

Many narratives, though, were authentic. A few were the work of former slaves who had learned to read and write as children or after reaching the North. Others were put together by writers who essentially wrote down what slaves told them. In either case, the events described in the books reflected the realities of slavery and the personal feelings of the slaves. They are extremely useful in providing modern-day readers with a sense of what it might have been like to be enslaved.

Slave narratives typically follow a standard format. Since the narratives were intended for an anti-slavery audience, the books usually began by describing the brutality of the slaveholders in detail. Most of the violence in the books consisted of whippings and beatings, but the narratives described more severe cruelty as well. In some cases, the narrators were brought to the brink of death at the hands of their tormentors. "The first thing he did was to pour some tar on my head," wrote Moses Roper about a particularly cruel white master, "then rubbed it all over my face ... and set it on fire."[19] Roper barely survived.

Following the graphic opening portions of slave narratives, the second section of most works described the slave's attempt to escape. This part of the narrative emphasized the physical and psychological terrors of the journey north toward freedom. Fugitives most often traveled by night, sneaking through forests and swamps and avoiding towns and main roads. They ran low on food, they suffered in cold and rain, and they knew that one mistake or one stroke of bad luck could result in capture. "I was hungry and began to feel the desperation of distress," wrote James Pennington about his challenging journey from bondage in Maryland to freedom in Pennsylvania. "As I travelled I felt my strength failing and my spirits wavered; my mind was in a deep and [sad] dream."[20] Accounts similar to this were standard in slave narratives.

The First Slave Narrative

The slave narrative genre got its start in 1789, when a British publisher printed the memoirs of a man named Olaudah Equiano (also known as Gustavus Vassa). Equiano's life story was considered well worth recording. According to his narrative, Equiano was born in West Africa about 1745. Kidnapped and sold into slavery at the age of 10 or 11, he served a variety of masters before being sold to white traders who eventually brought him to Virginia. Once in North America, Equiano impressed his owners with his talents and intelligence. Despite being a slave, he became literate and was taught business practices and navigational techniques. When Equiano reached his early 20s, he purchased his freedom, settled in England, and began campaigning for the end of slavery. He died in 1797.

Equiano's memoir, entitled *The Interesting Narrative of the Life of Olaudah Equiano, or Gustavus Vassa, the African*, was a financial success. It went through several printings in its first few years of publication, and it was widely read both in England and in the northern United States for many years thereafter. Its popularity was due to the book's quality. Equiano's life was, as the title boasted, interesting, and his story was well told, though its style is outdated by modern standards. It was dramatic, tragic, hopeful, and shocking. Equiano not only described the realities of his life, but gave a running account of his feelings as well. "All within my [heart] was tumult, wildness, and delirium!" Equiano wrote, reliving the moment when he finally acquired his freedom. "My feet scarcely touched the

Olaudah Equiano,
or
GUSTAVUS VASSA,
the African?

Published. March 1 1789 by G. Vassa

The Interesting Narrative of the Life of Olaudah Equiano, or Gustavus Vassa, the African *was the story of a man's harrowing experience as a slave, and it is still read by students and historians today.*

THE

INTERESTING NARRATIVE

OF

THE LIFE

OF

OLAUDAH EQUIANO,

OR

GUSTAVUS VASSA,

THE AFRICAN.

WRITTEN BY HIMSELF.

Behold, God is my salvation; I will trust, and not be afraid, for the Lord Jehovah is my strength and my song; he also is become my salvation.
And in that day shall ye say, Praise the Lord, call upon his name, declare his doings among the people. Isa. xii. 2. 4.

EIGHTH EDITION ENLARGED.

NORWICH:

PRINTED FOR, AND SOLD BY THE AUTHOR.

1794.

PRICE FOUR SHILLINGS.

Formerly sold for 7s.

[*Entered at Stationers' Hall.*]

ground, for they were winged with joy."[21]

Equiano's book had two main purposes. One was religious. A faithful Christian who had been baptized into the faith while still enslaved, Equiano frequently referred to his trust in God and to God's promise of heaven for believers. In this way, *The Interesting Narrative* was an evangelical document: Equiano intended to spread the message of Christian salvation among his readers. The second purpose, however, was political. As with later narratives, Equiano's work detailed and attacked the evils of slavery. He wanted to enrage and horrify his audience, encouraging them to join the fight for abolition. Accordingly, Equiano closed the book with a call to British officials to end England's involvement in the slave trade.

The Many Slave Narratives That Followed

Equiano's memoir set the stage for later slave narratives. Like Equiano's account, the narratives of the 19th century were often both religious and political. They included long descriptions of the evils of slavery, but they also assured readers of the mercy of a Christian God—both as a tool for evangelism and as a way to link the antislavery cause with Christian ideals. There were other similarities, too. Just as Equiano's book was packed with drama and suspense, so too were the works of later narrators. Nearly every narrative, regardless of when it was published, ended on a positive note, with the author gaining their freedom and leaving slavery behind forever.

There were two points, however, in which later narratives differed from Equiano's. For one, Equiano's memoir described his childhood in Africa and his terrifying journey across the Atlantic Ocean. These events were missing from most 19th century slave narratives because the authors of these works had typically been born in North America and had no direct connection to an African homeland. The other difference had to do with how the narrators achieved their freedom. Equiano bought his freedom, but few later writers did the same.

Slave narratives included dramatic accounts of the dangers faced during an escape from slavery and made for compelling and popular books.

AMERICAN POET

James M. Whitfield was an African American born in New Hampshire in 1822. Whitfield worked as a barber much of his life, but his true interest was poetry. In 1853, he published a collection of poems titled *American and Other Poems* that summed up the anger many northern blacks of the time felt toward the United States and its white citizens for their treatment of African Americans. It began,

America, it is to thee
Thou boasted land of liberty,—
It is to thee I raise my song,
Thou land of blood, and crime,
and wrong.[1]

Whitfield went on to describe the cruelty of taking black people from Africa to labor as slaves, also discussing the brutality with which most slaves were treated. African Americans, he concluded, had been

Stripped of those rights which
Nature's God
Bequeathed to all the
human race,
Bound to a petty tyrant's nod,
Because he wears a
paler face.[2]

1. James Monroe Whitfield, "America," Academy of American Poets, accessed May 18, 2017. www.poets.org/poetsorg/poem/america-3.

2. Whitfield, "America."

Dozens of American poets opposed slavery, including John Greenleaf Whittier, whose poetry is shown here.

Most often, they ran away from their homes and owners, leaving their former lives behind in a dangerous and often dramatic quest for freedom.

Indeed, the descriptions of escapes in the slave narratives of the 1800s are astonishing. In 1860, for instance, former slaves William and Ellen Craft published a book titled *Running a Thousand Miles for Freedom*. The text focused on the Crafts' bold escape by train from the slave state of Georgia to the free state of Pennsylvania. Ellen, a light-skinned black woman, disguised herself as a young white man, a southern planter traveling to Philadelphia, Pennsylvania, for a medical consultation. William, much darker than his wife, played the role of the young planter's slave. After several narrow escapes, including a moment when Ellen—who could neither read nor write—was asked to sign a document, the couple finally arrived in Pennsylvania.

A similarly dramatic tale involved a Virginia slave named Henry Brown. Resolving to escape after his wife and children were separated from him, Brown had friends pack him inside a small crate and mail him to a northern antislavery society. The trip, completed mainly by train, was excruciating. During the journey, which took more than one full day, Brown had little fresh air, hardly any room to move, and practically no food or water. The psychological horror may have been even worse than the physical discomfort. "A cold sweat now covered me from head to foot," he wrote at one point in his narrative. "Death seemed my inevitable fate."[22] Despite the challenges, Brown survived and reached his destination. He became known as "Box" Brown, and his account of the escape was published in both England and America.

The Most Famous African American of His Time

Probably the best known of all slave narratives—and the most "literary" as well—was a book titled *Narrative of the Life of Frederick Douglass, an American Slave*. Douglass, who wrote the book without any assistance, was one of the most remarkable Americans—of any race—in history. Born into slavery in Maryland in about 1818, Douglass learned to read as a boy. As a young adult, Douglass decided to run north to freedom. Though his first few attempts were unsuccessful, he reached New York in 1838. He went on to become a famous abolitionist

Frederick Douglass was a talented writer whose autobiography is still popular today.

and political leader who was espe-cially famous for his public-speaking abilities. It is likely that he was the most famous African American of his time.

Douglass published his autobi-ography in 1845. In some ways, Douglass's narrative was like others in the genre. For example, Douglass described the brutal punishments he received at the hands of his mas-ters, and he was not afraid to write about the horrifying realities of slavery. Douglass also described his desire for freedom, though his nar-rative was not specific regarding the details of his final, successful escape attempt. He feared that a thorough description would give white mas-ters too much information about how to hunt down slaves, which would hurt others who wanted to make escapes of their own.

Although there were many simi-larities, Douglass's autobiography did differ from the standard slave narra-tives of the day. One was Douglass's exceptional writing skill. He wrote in clear, careful prose, resulting in a book of such quality that some prejudiced critics doubted that Douglass was the actual author. Moreover, Douglass's memoir moved beyond the relatively simple discus-sions of slavery and faith prominent in most slave narratives. While Douglass was a devout Christian, he viewed his religion more critically than most. In particular, he drew a sharp line between what he perceived as Christian ideals and the practices of the slave-holders. "I love the pure, peaceable, and impartial Christianity of Christ," he wrote. "I therefore hate the corrupt, slaveholding, women-whipping, cradle-plundering, partial and hypocritical Christianity of this land."[23]

Douglass's subtly distinct atti-tudes were evident in other areas as well. His autobiography took up complex questions of racism, patri-otism, and more—themes that also appeared in Douglass's later writings and speeches. Many of Douglass's words echoed those of black writers, such as Walker and Delany. While these earlier writers were read primarily by African Americans, Douglass brought similar ideas to audiences who were largely white. "What, to the American slave, is your 4th of July?" he asked white listeners in an 1852 speech. "To him, your celebration is a sham ... your shouts of liberty and equality [are a] hollow mockery."[24] Slave narratives rarely attacked American society in general like this. Most preferred, instead, to blame southern whites alone. As Douglass saw it, however,

INCIDENTS IN THE LIFE OF A SLAVE GIRL

In 1861, the year the Civil War began, a woman named Harriet Jacobs published a book titled *Incidents in the Life of a Slave Girl*. Using the pseudonym Linda Brent, Jacobs described the horrifying details of her life growing up in slavery. The book's importance lies partly in its open discussion of Jacobs's own experiences, but it is also valuable for the insight it gives into the problems faced by many slave women. In particular, the book tells of Jacobs's desperate attempts to protect herself from being raped by her owner and her sorrow and frustration at being unable to protect her children from harm. Both experiences were common for slave women across the South.

Jacobs described the horror of her everyday life under Dr. Flint, her master:

My master met me at every turn, reminding me that I belonged to him, and swearing by heaven and earth that he would compel me to submit to him. If I went out for a breath of fresh air, after a day of unwearied toil, his footsteps [followed] me. If I knelt by my mother's grave, his dark shadow fell on me even there. The light heart which nature had given me became heavy with sad [thoughts] ... I longed for some one to confide in. I would have given the world to have laid my head on my grandmother's faithful bosom, and told her all my troubles. But Dr. Flint swore he would kill me, if I was not as silent as the grave.[1]

1. Harriet Jacobs. *Incidents in the Life of a Slave Girl*. Boston, MA: Harriet Jacobs, 1861, p. 46.

all of America was part of slavery. Whether this idea was popular with his audiences or not, he thought it was necessary to say and write what he believed.

The Political Power of Literature

From a literary perspective, the writings of Douglass, Walker, Equiano, and other African Americans of the early 1800s were undoubtedly important. Douglass, in particular, was a remarkable writer whose eloquence is as evident today as it was in the 1840s. Walker and Garnet made excellent use of clear, plain language and intelligent rhetorical devices to stir up their readers. Equiano, together with some other former slaves, not only invented a new genre, but also wrote scenes of drama and suspense that rank among the most stirring of their time.

The best of these works added to the richness of the African American literary tradition and brought black literature more fully into the mainstream of American writing as well. By exploring important moral, philosophical, and political questions, these writers captured the attention—and in many cases, the respect and admiration—of northern whites. At the time of the American Revolution, white Americans frequently dismissed the idea that black Americans could be authors. By the time of the Civil War, whites were more willing to accept that African Americans could produce literature—and some even acknowledged that their works were outstanding.

As important as the writings of these authors are to African American literature, their main significance lies in their impact on American history. Many factors led to the eventual abolition of slavery following the Civil War, but among these factors was the rapid growth of the antislavery movement in the North in the 1840s and 1850s. The increasingly passionate and logical arguments against slavery not only helped bring many northerners to abolition, but also caused southern whites to respond in ways that brought about war between the two sections of the country—a war that eventually destroyed the slave system in America. The writings of Douglass, Harper, the Crafts, and other black authors were instrumental in spreading the abolitionist message and, by extension, were instrumental in bringing about the end of slavery. That is their greatest legacy.

CHAPTER THREE

POSTBELLUM STORIES: 1865–1918

In 1865, the abolitionists, assisted by the voices of African American writers from earlier decades, finally achieved their aim: The institution of slavery was ended in the United States. However, the period after the Civil War, sometimes called the postbellum period, was not an easy one for African Americans. Although the direct evil of slavery was over, it left behind a harmful legacy of poverty, racism, and a lack of education and opportunity. African Americans, even after slavery was abolished, had limited options, and the South was a difficult place to be. Laws were quickly passed to further limit the options of former slaves and establish segregation, or separation, based on race. Black writers in the late 1800s and early 1900s continued to speak out against these injustices.

Novels About Black Life

Prior to the Civil War, nonfiction was the most common genre used by black authors. Writers such as Frederick Douglass, David Walker, and Olaudah Equiano made excellent use of autobiographical accounts and persuasive essays to express their ideas. In contrast, Phillis Wheatley and Frances Harper were among only a few black writers to publish fiction or poetry. Following the Civil War, however, the heavy focus on nonfiction began to change. Though autobiographies and essays remained popular, a significant number of African American authors began producing poems, stories, and novels. In some ways, the period following the Civil War marks the beginning of black fiction and other genres.

The most famous African

After the Civil War, Charles Chesnutt emerged as one of the leading voices in African American literature; he is still regarded for his powerful novels.

American writer of fiction in the late 19th century was an Ohio native named Charles W. Chesnutt. Born in 1858, Chesnutt published several novels and dozens of short stories. Chesnutt's fiction most often described the lives of ordinary black men and women, and he was especially interested in themes of black culture and traditions. Several of his stories discuss the superstitions and religious practices of rural African Americans. Others are based in part on tales from black folklore.

Unlike many previous writers, Chesnutt was not overtly political. That did not mean, however, that he ignored issues of poverty or racism on the national level. On the contrary, Chesnutt used his fictional characters to make important political and social points. His 1899 book *The Conjure Woman*, for example, is largely made up of stories told by a former slave to a white couple who had moved south following the Civil War. Many of the stories date from the days of slavery, and several clearly demonstrate the brutality of the slave era. The narrator rarely reveals his feelings about these stories, but Chesnutt does not hesitate to show the white couple's reactions of disgust. By having this criticism come from a white outsider rather than from a black participant, Chesnutt made the criticism of slavery more powerful for white audiences.

Chesnutt also used humor and satire to deliver deeper messages. One of his stories tells of Dick Owens, the grown son of a wealthy slave owner in the years just before the Civil War. To impress his girlfriend, who believes him to be lazy, Dick resolves to do something daring: He will help Grandison, one of his father's many slaves, escape to Canada. He plans a tour of the North and talks his father into sending Grandison along as Dick's personal servant.

Grandison seems surprisingly content to be a slave. He spends his days bowing and grinning and assuring Dick that the free blacks of the North were worse than the enslaved blacks of the South. Still, Dick assumes that Grandison will run away the moment he has an opportunity—and Dick plans to give the young slave as many opportunities as necessary. Once in the North, however, Grandison repeatedly fails to run off. Claiming to have a fear of abolitionists and utter loyalty to his masters, he refuses to leave. Dick is eventually forced to lead Grandison into Canadian territory and walk

SONGS ABOUT HARD TIMES

The blues was a musical form created by African Americans at the end of the 1800s and in the early 1900s. The traditional blues song uses a series of rhyming lyrics to describe feelings or a situation. Most blues songs focus on hardship and pain; common themes in blues lyrics include broken hearts, a lack of money, and the day-to-day difficulty of staying alive in a world that does not seem to care. Today, the entire genre of blues is often seen as a uniquely African American art form.

Some blues songs have a single composer. W.C. Handy, a black bandleader from Alabama, was one of the earliest and most influential of these. He wrote the words and music to blues classics such as "Memphis Blues," "Yellow Dog Blues," and the well-known "St. Louis Blues." Handy's connection to the blues is so strong, in fact, that he titled his autobiography *Father of the Blues*.

Though some blues songs were written by individual artists such as Handy, many others were created through a more complicated process: passing the songs on from one performer to another, each person making a few changes before passing it along. The blues has never given up its hold on American popular musical styles. Though it originated with rural African Americans in the years after the Civil War, it has expanded to be accessible to people of all races well into the 21st century.

away when the slave is not looking.

A month after Dick returns home, however, Grandison appears on the doorstep. Why Grandison would voluntarily return to slavery is a mystery to Dick at first. One night a few weeks later, though, all becomes clear when Grandison disappears—and not just Grandison, but his wife, his parents, and his siblings as well. Grandison quickly leads his family members into Canada, following the route Dick unwittingly showed him. By pretending to be what he was not on the original trip, Grandison freed not just himself, but his entire family. The lesson of Chesnutt's story echoes a common lesson in black folklore dating all the way back to Br'er Rabbit: Despite a lack of power, black people can still outwit their white oppressors.

Postbellum Poetry

Chesnutt was the leading African

American novelist of the late 1800s, but the leading African American poet of the time was a man named Paul Laurence Dunbar. Like Chesnutt, Dunbar was a native of Ohio. Born in 1872, Dunbar shared Chesnutt's interest in black culture and traditions, and much of his poetry celebrates this interest. An excellent example is a poem titled "When Malindy Sings," which describes the singing voice of Malindy, a fictional African American woman. The poem honors the role of music in African American society and makes it clear that African Americans are more than capable of producing great art.

Dunbar also wrote of the struggles faced by black people as they tried to make their way in a world run largely by whites. One of his most famous works, "We Wear the Mask," discusses the need for blacks to cover their true selves when dealing with the white majority. During this period, whites typically expected African Americans to act happy and cheerful. Fearful of the consequences of showing other emotions, especially anger, blacks commonly obeyed. To Dunbar, this was similar to putting on a mask that made it impossible

to see the wearer clearly.

Dunbar's concern was that the mask made it impossible for white people to see black people for who they really were. His deeper worry was the effect this mask had on the African Americans who metaphorically wore it. The psychological damage of not being able to express feelings, Dunbar argued, is appalling. As he wrote in the poem's conclusion,

> We smile, but, O great Christ,
>   our cries
> To thee from tortured souls arise.
> We sing, but oh the clay is vile
> Beneath our feet, and long
>   the mile;
> But let the world dream
>   otherwise,
>   We wear the mask![25]

Respect for History

Dunbar was not the only African American to earn widespread attention for his poetry. He was joined by one of his contemporaries, a writer named James Weldon Johnson. Born in Florida in 1871, Johnson was gifted in many areas besides poetry. Throughout his life, he was a schoolteacher, a college professor, and a book editor;

he also wrote songs, worked for the U.S. government, and served as president of a black political organization. During his lifetime, he was widely recognized as one of the most talented figures of black America, and today he is often considered one of the top minds of his generation.

Like both Chesnutt and Dunbar, Johnson had a deep interest in black folklore, culture, and history, and these themes are at the center of most of Johnson's work. He is mainly known today for a 1908 poem that celebrates black spirituals. To Johnson, the spirituals—both words and music—represented one of the greatest artistic achievements of the New World. Johnson found the creation of the spirituals especially remarkable given that these works had been created by the victims of slavery.

Johnson believed African Americans needed to embrace their unique history. Accordingly, he edited one of the first books of African American poetry and wrote several important essays about the African American past. He also wrote an influential poem, "Lift Ev'ry Voice and Sing," which focused on the black past and present. First published as a poem in 1900 and later set to music by Johnson's brother Rosamond, the poem urges African Americans to understand and take pride in their heritage. Throughout the work, Johnson acknowledges the obstacles African Americans faced throughout their history. At the same time, the poem is optimistic. Johnson believed that since slavery had been dismantled, the natural abilities of African Americans would be able to flourish across the nation. Moreover, he reassures his audience that Christianity and God were on the side of black Americans, just as other contemporary authors did.

In the years since it was written, "Lift Ev'ry Voice and Sing" has inspired and comforted generations of African Americans. It is frequently sung in churches as a hymn, and even in the 21st century, it remains a common feature of meetings and celebrations held in black communities. Johnson's understanding of the trials and beauty of African American history, together with his message to look to the future with hope and anticipation, gave his poem strength and depth. Even now, more than a century after it was written, the piece is a classic of African American literature.

James Weldon Johnson was a talented poet who took inspiration from the oral traditions of African American literature.

AN IMPORTANT SCHOOL

Booker T. Washington believed wholeheartedly that African Americans' greatest responsibility was to improve their communities. As an educator, Washington urged his students to return to their hometowns rather than seeking their fortunes in the large cities of the South. In this excerpt from his influential autobiography *Up from Slavery*, Washington explains his goal for his students at Tuskegee Normal and Industrial Institute, the school he founded in Alabama:

We found that the most of our students came from the country districts, where agriculture in some form or other was the main dependence of the people. We learned that about eighty-five per cent of the coloured people in the Gulf states depended upon agriculture for their living. Since this was true, we wanted to be careful not to educate our students out of sympathy with agricultural life, so that they would be attracted from the country to the cities, and yield to the temptation of trying to live by their wits. We wanted to give them such an education as would fit a large proportion of them to be teachers, and at the same time cause them to return to the plantation districts and show the people there how to put new energy and new ideas into farming, as well as into the intellectual and moral and religious life of the people.[1]

Although some of Washington's ideas are out of fashion today, *Up from Slavery* remains a classic of American literature.

1. Booker T. Washington, *Up from Slavery.* New York, NY: Doubleday, 1901, p. 59.

Booker T. Washington was an author and powerful intellectual in the years after the Civil War.

THE LASTING IMPACT OF JAMES WELDON JOHNSON'S WORDS

In this excerpt from Maya Angelou's memoir *I Know Why the Caged Bird Sings*, Angelou recalls the pride she and her classmates felt while singing James Weldon Johnson's "Lift Ev'ry Voice and Sing" at her eighth grade graduation from a segregated school in rural Arkansas:

Every child I knew had learned that song with his ABC's and along with "Jesus Loves Me This I Know." But I personally had never heard it before. Never heard the words, despite the thousands of times I had sung them. Never thought they had anything to do with me ... And now I heard, really for the first time:

*"We have come over a way that with tears
has been watered,
We have come, treading our path through
the blood of the slaughtered." ...*

We were on top again. As always, again. We survived. The depths had been icy and dark, but now a proud sun spoke to our souls. I was no longer simply a member of the proud graduating class of 1940; I was a proud member of the wonderful, beautiful Negro race.[1]

1. Maya Angelou. *I Know Why the Caged Bird Sings.* New York, NY: Random House, 1969, pp. 181–182.

Postbellum Nonfiction

Though fiction and poetry were becoming a vital part of African American literature after the Civil War, nonfiction remained one of the most popular genres. Several prominent African Americans wrote essays, autobiographical accounts, and histories during this period. Chief among these writers were two men whose backgrounds, personalities, and outlooks were very different, but who shared a desire to improve the lives of African Americans everywhere. One of these men was Booker T. Washington; the other, W.E.B. DuBois. The most influential black writers of their time, Washington and DuBois served in many ways as the political, cultural, and moral leaders of black America in the period between the Civil War and World War I.

The older of these two men, Washington was born into slavery on a Virginia plantation in 1856. From early on, he recognized that even free blacks were not treated as full members of society. As an adult, he resolved to try to change that. Washington hoped that white leaders would someday be ready to accept blacks as their political and social equals. At the same time, Washington was a realist, and he suspected that such acceptance was a long way off. Rather than push for voting rights, an immediate end to segregation, and other political changes, Washington decided to use another strategy: education.

In 1891, Washington moved to Alabama and became the founding president of Tuskegee Normal and Industrial Institute. This school was designed to prepare African Americans for jobs in business, agriculture, and manufacturing. As Washington saw it, job training was essential to any effort to improve the lives of African Americans. Better job skills, he noted, would increase the earning power of blacks and would help African Americans move out of poverty. It would also show whites that African Americans could be more than farmhands and unskilled laborers. Once African Americans became economically self-sufficient, Washington argued, campaigns to establish broader civil rights might be successful. In the meantime, however, working toward these goals would have to wait.

"Mutual Progress"

In 1895, Washington presented his ideas in a speech to an integrated audience at an Atlanta business convention. "In all things that are purely social, [blacks and whites] can be as separate as the fingers," Washington said, "yet one as the hand in all things essential to mutual progress."[26] The speech immediately brought Washington into the national spotlight and solidified his role as a leader of African Americans. Whites approved of his willingness not to press for immediate political and social rights; many blacks applauded Washington's determination to increase their standard of living. Almost overnight, Washington became nationally famous.

Over the next few years, Washington worked tirelessly for African American economic self-sufficiency. He lectured, wrote, and traveled widely to bring his message to blacks and whites across the country. In 1901, he published the most significant of his works, an autobiography titled *Up from Slavery*. The book reflected Washington's general policy of emphasizing what blacks could do for themselves rather than complaining about the evils of society. Even at the beginning of the narrative, Washington took pains to point out that although he and his fellow slaves had reacted joyfully to the news that they were finally free, they were not going to hold a grudge against their former masters.

Up from Slavery went on to describe Washington's education, his leadership at the Tuskegee Normal and Industrial Institute, and the speech that had brought him national attention. It also made clear Washington's basic philosophy. "I believe it is the duty of the Negro," he wrote, "to [act] modestly in regard to political claims ... I think that the according of the full exercise of political rights is going to be a matter of natural, slow growth."[27] Popular among whites as well as many blacks, Washington's autobiography was effective and influential. It set a tone for public debate on racial issues—not only for the time, but for many years to come. *Up from Slavery* remains one of the great works of African American literature.

A Call for Full Citizenship

If Washington represented one type of black leader, DuBois—born in Massachusetts in 1868—represented the opposite extreme. As a scholar, political activist, and editor, DuBois passionately disagreed with Washington's willingness to wait for social and political equality. DuBois argued that Washington's methods would never lead to full civil rights for blacks. To him, political change was the first and most important goal. "By every civilized and peaceful method," DuBois wrote in a direct attack on Washington and his policies, "we must strive for the rights which the world accords to men."[28]

In 1903, DuBois published a book of essays titled *The Souls of Black Folk*. Many of the essays described his approach to the problem of racism. In contrast to Washington, DuBois demanded basic rights for African Americans, and he demanded them without delay. In his eyes, black leaders were obligated to push for these rights. Much of *The Souls of Black Folk* was dedicated to DuBois's opinions on this subject and his disagreements—sometimes sharp, sometimes more mild—with Washington and other blacks who adopted his perspective.

Like *Up from Slavery*, though, *The Souls of Black Folk* was much more than a political document. Many African Americans found that the book captured their experience of being black in an overwhelmingly white world. Many found that DuBois described their sorrows and their dreams; he understood and accepted both the challenges and the joys of being African American. Blacks, DuBois wrote at one point, had a "sense of always looking at one's self through the eyes of others, of measuring one's soul by the tape of a world that looks on in amused contempt and pity."[29]

Into the Future

Washington died in 1915, but DuBois continued his advocacy for African Americans for decades to come. He lived until 1963, leaving behind dozens of writings about politics, history, and what it means to be black. Today, most black critics hold DuBois's work in higher esteem than they do Washington's, believing that the passage of time has demonstrated that DuBois's ideas were more effective than Washington's. DuBois stands out as one of the giants of African American literature—and of American history, as well.

DuBois is not alone in this distinction. Washington's memoir, though not as politically persuasive as it once was, remains an inspiring tale of a man who rose from slavery to become a leader of his people. From the folkloric images of Chesnutt's *The Conjure Woman* to the racial pride of Johnson's poetry and from the political wisdom of DuBois to the keen insight of Dunbar, African American literature had come a long way since

W. E. B. DuBois wrote The Souls of Black Folk, *a collection of political essays calling for equal rights for African Americans.*

the early works of Phillis Wheatley and Jupiter Hammon. It had broadened its focus, branched into new literary forms, and come to appeal more and more to a broad and diverse audience. Perhaps most of all, black literature of this period had become ever more supportive and reflective of the black experience. The works of 18th century African American authors had brought black literature to a new level. The next generations of African American writers would take these themes and develop them further still.

CHAPTER FOUR

NEW YORK CITY STORIES: 1918–1940

One of the most creative periods in African American literature took place in New York City in the 1920s. Known as the Harlem Renaissance, this artistic movement catapulted black authors into a broader global spotlight. This period of history brought more options, greater economic opportunity, and more room for diverse voices in American culture. African American authors came together and amplified each other's voices. Many of the authors from this period enjoyed great popularity during their day.

The Harlem Renaissance took its name from the Harlem neighborhood of New York City, which has historically had a large black population. Many African American artists moved to Harlem to create and share novels, poetry, visual art, and music. This fertile creative period began in the 1920s and marked the beginning of modern African American literature. The writers of the Harlem Renaissance supported one another, published widely, and broke out onto the larger American literary stage.

A Destination for Artists

Located on the northern part of Manhattan Island, Harlem became a destination for African Americans in the early 1900s. Black men and women who already lived in New York City were attracted to the neighborhood's wide streets, solid houses, and relatively low rents. Black migrants from the rural South, searching for better lives and higher-paying jobs, also settled in the community. Between 1920 and 1930, the number of African Americans living in Harlem skyrocketed.

Many of Harlem's new African American residents were poor and uneducated. They managed to create a meager living by working for low wages as laborers or servants. Harlem also attracted well-educated black residents. These men and women viewed the neighborhood as something unique: a place within the country's biggest metropolis where African Americans of every background could join together and build a new and exciting community. As James Weldon Johnson wrote in 1925, "Harlem is not merely a Negro colony or community, it is a city within a city, the greatest Negro city in the world."[30] By the early 1920s, the community had become established as a

The Harlem neighborhood of New York City was largely populated by African Americans; it was a logical birthplace for a new era of black literature.

center of African American culture. In Harlem, many African Americans felt they could embrace their history and culture to create a new, exciting identity. The literature that came out of Harlem reflected this sense of excitement in many ways.

Breaking Down Publishing Barriers

The person perhaps most responsible for the Harlem Renaissance was an African American scholar named Charles S. Johnson. Born in 1893, Johnson was a sociologist by training, and he was a strong advocate against racism at a time when few black people felt safe speaking out. In the early 1920s, Johnson came to Harlem to work for a black advocacy group named the National Urban League. One of his duties was to edit the organization's new magazine, *Opportunity: Journal of Negro Life*. At first, Johnson filled the magazine with scholarly articles. Soon after, though, he decided to instead emphasize the arts. *Opportunity* began to publish short stories and poems written by up-and-coming black authors, along with theater reviews and other articles about the arts.

Johnson was impressed with the talents of the people he recruited to write for his magazine, and he decid-ed to bring their work to the attention of white publishers. Though few mainstream presses had printed fiction or poetry by black writers in the past, Johnson believed that the new generation of publishers might be ready to change this policy. Johnson's academic background and work with the National Urban League gave him connections to influential members of white society. Johnson was in the perfect situation to bring African American writing into the broader literary culture.

In March 1924, Johnson hosted a party to celebrate the publication of a novel by a Harlem writer and editor named Jessie Fauset. The guests included many of the most promising young writers in Harlem, along with veteran authors such as W. E. B. DuBois. However, not all the guests were African American. He had invited white authors and publishers as well, and several of these men were in attendance. Johnson hoped that the white guests would be impressed by the black writers they met and consider publishing some of their works.

In this goal, Johnson was wildly successful. At the party, a white editor named Carl Van Doren gave a speech in which he strongly urged white publishers to seek out black authors. "What American literature

CANE

Jean Toomer, a mixed-race poet and novelist, was born in the Washington, D.C., in 1894. Toomer was a major figure in the Harlem Renaissance. He was best known for a novel published in 1923 that he titled *Cane*. This unique novel included descriptions of black life in the rural South, as well as in the urban North. Lyrically written and moving back and forth between prose, poetry, and drama, *Cane* was an immediate success; critics praised the novel for its realistic depiction of African American culture and its beautiful language. Though not read as often today as when it was first published, it remains a classic of black literature.

Oddly, though, *Cane*'s author was never comfortable with his racial heritage. He resisted being classified as a black writer. In his essays, especially those published after *Cane*, Toomer argued that he was both black and white, not simply African American, as most people perceived him. On one occasion, in fact, he described his ancestry as a blend of various European ethnic groups—and then added that he carried some African heritage as well. It is unclear why he tried so hard to reject his African American ties. Despite his attempt to carve a racial identity of his own, Toomer is still recognized as an important figure in the Harlem Renaissance, as well as one of the finest black writers of his time.

Jean Toomer was the author of an experimental novel, Cane, *which mixed together prose, poetry, and drama.*

decidedly needs at this moment is color, music, [and] gusto," he argued. "If the Negroes are not in a position to contribute these items, I do not know what Americans are."[31] Agreeing with Van Doren's suggestion, many publishers and editors at the party showed great interest in learning more about Harlem's writers and their work. The editor of *Harper's Magazine* went even further: After hearing a young writer named Countee Cullen read some of his poetry at the celebration, he immediately agreed to publish Cullen's work in an upcoming issue.

Despite the noticeable interest created at Johnson's party, the Harlem Renaissance did not begin on that night. To a large degree, the movement had already been in development for years. Most of the authors who made their names during the movement were already writing, and some, like Fauset, had achieved recognition for their work. Still, that evening in 1924 brought the movement into the public eye, attracted new writers to Harlem, and helped establish a connection among the literary figures of the black community. Over the next few years, encouraged by Johnson and a black editor named Alain Locke, Harlem-based writers sold their novels to white publishers and placed their poetry and essays in national magazines. A barrier had been broken, and the Harlem Renaissance was underway.

Many Voices

The Harlem Renaissance is a difficult movement to characterize. In one sense, the movement was quite cohesive. The writers who made up the movement largely viewed themselves as being part of a group. Many of them lived within just a few miles of each other. They moved in the same social and professional circles; they supported each other's work; and they pushed as a unit for greater recognition in the black community and beyond.

At the same time, however, the works produced by these writers often had very little in common with one another. The men and women of the Harlem Renaissance wrote in various distinct genres and made use of an enormous number of literary forms and styles. Cullen was best known for his poetry, Fauset for her novels. Zora Neale Hurston, born in Alabama in 1891, was trained as a folklorist; her works include collections of traditional African American tales. Langston Hughes, an exceptionally versatile writer, published poetry, novels, short stories, plays, and nonfiction. While some literary movements in American history have

Zora Neale Hurston found success bringing the grit and realism of poor black life to her novels.

they were all black, they had different experiences, interests, and backgrounds, and sometimes the differences in upbringing were great indeed. Wealth, education, and social status, for example, were important dividers. Cullen, for example, grew up in an upper–middle class Harlem household as the son of a respected minister. Hughes, in contrast, grew up poor; his father abandoned his family, and Hughes was raised by his grandmother while his mother traveled to find work. Cullen earned a graduate degree, while many other writers of the movement lacked a degree at all.

Geographic origin divided the writers of the Harlem Renaissance as well. Some, such as Cullen, came from the East, while Hughes was a midwesterner, and Hurston grew up in the South. Many came from New York; Los Angeles, California; or other urban areas, but others grew up in small towns or even in rural areas. Geography affected racial diversity as well. Hurston was raised in a

focused on a specific genre, such as drama, poems, or essays, the Harlem Renaissance included all of these and more.

These disparities made sense. The writers of the Harlem Renaissance were not all alike by any means. Though

Nella Larsen (second from left) is shown here winning a prize for her literary work.

community populated entirely by African Americans, whereas Hughes was one of just two black students in his eighth-grade class.

For that matter, some of the writers of the Harlem Renaissance had roots outside the United States. Poet and novelist Claude McKay, for example, was born and raised in Jamaica and did not come to the United States until his early 20s. Novelist Nella Larsen, the child of a white European mother and a black father from the Caribbean, grew up partly in the United States and partly in Denmark.

Given the differences in geography, education, background, and experience, it is easy to understand why the Harlem Renaissance represented such a variety of styles and genres despite having a common theme: uplifting African Americans.

Style

The diversity of styles is not hard to see. Cullen's poetry, for example, uses traditional structure and language. Many of his poems are sonnets, a strict 14-line form used by John Keats, William Shakespeare, and countless other English poets. Cullen's sonnets are easily distinguishable from those of Keats or Shakespeare because of their topics and themes. "Yet do I marvel at this curious thing," he wrote in one sonnet, "To make a poet black, and bid him sing!"[32] In style and structure, though, Cullen's poetry was directly in line with the traditional form.

Compared with Cullen and several other writers of the Harlem Renaissance, Hughes was much more experimental in his approach to poetry. Hughes was best known for his free verse—poetry in which rhyme and meter are not important. Even in his earliest work, Hughes was already playing with new structures and ideas. His first published poem, printed when Hughes was still a teenager, ended with the lines

I've known rivers:
Ancient, dusky rivers.

My soul has grown deep like
*   the rivers.*[33]

Some poets of the period made extensive use of artistic forms from black culture. The blues, for example, was a relatively new musical style in the early 1920s. Associated mostly with black musicians in Mississippi and nearby parts of the South, it had spread into northern cities by the time the Harlem Renaissance began. Blues lyrics commonly focused on the difficulties of life, and blues songs followed a rigid, almost standardized format. Several of the best-known poems of the Harlem Renaissance, including Hughes's "The Weary Blues," were written in this new style, which was quickly identified as African American.

Just as the forms and styles varied from one poet to the next, the structures and subjects used by novelists of the Harlem Renaissance differed as well. Some writers, such as Fauset, wrote largely about well-off and influential blacks in cities such as Philadelphia and New York. Others, such as Hurston, were more inclined to write about the lives of African Americans in the rural South. Still others, notably McKay, focused their attention on lower-class blacks in urban areas.

Each of these writers, however, used dialogue that matched their characters' lives. The well-educated people of Fauset's work, for instance, use standard English, while the characters in Hurston's and McKay's books use expressions and grammatical constructions typical of lower-class blacks of the time. "Ah

PRIZES FOR POETRY

Langston Hughes was first published in 1921, shortly before his 20th birthday, when his poem "The Negro Speaks of Rivers" appeared in the magazine *Crisis*. Though the poem is recognized as a classic today, it did not bring Hughes instant fame—or much fame at all. Over the next few years, in fact, Hughes had difficulty getting anything else published. Between 1921 and 1925, he worked at a variety of unskilled jobs, writing when time permitted and hoping to be able to make a living as a writer someday.

In 1925, Hughes was working in the dining room of a Washington hotel. One of the hotel's guests that year was a noted American poet named Vachel Lindsay. Eager for feedback on his work, and excited to make contacts within the writing world, Hughes approached Lindsay one evening as the guest ate. He handed Lindsay a sampling of his own poetry and asked for the poet's reaction. Though annoyed by the interruption, Lindsay agreed to read Hughes's work—and was deeply impressed.

Lindsay's support helped boost Hughes's confidence. Later that year, Hughes entered a poetry contest sponsored by another African American publication, *Opportunity*. Hughes's poem "The Weary Blues" won first prize, finally bringing him the attention he sought.

ain't been near de place, man," says one character in Hurston's novel *Their Eyes Were Watching God*. "Ah been down tuh de lake tryin' tuh ketch me uh fish."[34]

Writing About Race

Despite all the diversity of the Harlem Renaissance, one powerful similarity linked the work of every one of the men and women who were part of the movement: race. The writers of the Harlem Renaissance were all of African descent, and in a racist nation, this fact was of profound importance. Fauset and McKay, Hughes and Larsen—all were viewed as blacks first and writers second. Accordingly, the works of virtually every member of the movement discuss the experience of being black in America.

No two writers approached the theme of race in exactly the same way. Some wrote from a deeply political perspective. Their works lashed out at

America and the laws and traditions that constricted opportunities for blacks. McKay was more radical than most, including angry and bitter language in most of his works, but other writers of the movement echoed his sentiments. Hughes, who eventually arose as one of the most famous of the Harlem Renaissance authors, allowed some dissatisfaction to come through in his vibrant poems.

Other works instead emphasized the struggles of African Americans. Sometimes these struggles stemmed from the racism of powerful whites who saw no need to treat blacks humanely. "Cora, bake three cakes for Mary's birthday tomorrow night," demands a white employer in a Hughes short story about an African American maid. "You Cora, give Rover a bath in that tar soap I bought."[35] Sometimes, though, the struggles had little direct

Langston Hughes's poetry celebrated African American culture and was often hopeful that the future would bring less prejudice.

relationship to white racism. Several novels of the period, for example, describe the damage caused to African American communities by prostitution, alcoholism, and drug use.

Still other writings of the Harlem Renaissance focused on celebrating blacks and black culture. These stories and poems portray African American traditions in a positive light and encouraged black readers to take pride in their racial identity. In "I, Too," a poem by Hughes, after comparing the African American experience to the feelings of children refused seats at the dinner table, Hughes foresees a different attitude in years ahead. "They'll see how beautiful I am," the narrator predicts confidently, referring to prejudiced whites, "and be ashamed."[36] Another example is Larsen's novel *Passing*. The mixed-race central character in the novel pretends at first to have no African ancestry at all but ultimately embraces her black heritage. "You don't know, you can't realize how I want to see Negroes," she tells a friend, "to be with them again, to talk with them, to hear them laugh."[37]

No writer of the period played up the theme of black pride more than Hurston. Hurston's fiction is full of black characters who, though flawed, also have great strengths. Hurston tells her black readers again and again that African Americans can be strong, smart, and brave and being African American is something to take pride in—not something to be hidden or ashamed of. Her story "Drenched in Light," for instance, tells of a young black girl named Isis, whose happiness and purity make a deep impression on a wealthy white woman. "I want brightness and this Isis is joy itself," the woman exclaims. "Why she's drenched in light!"[38]

In keeping with their emphasis on race, many writers of the Harlem Renaissance looked to Africa for inspiration and identity. Despite their attraction to Africa, however, most writers of the movement ultimately saw themselves as Americans. Hughes, who visited Africa in the early 1920s, recognized that Africa was not the place that had shaped him. "I was ... an American Negro—who had loved the surface of Africa and the rhythms of Africa—but I was not Africa, I was Chicago and Kansas City and Broadway and Harlem."[39]

A Broad Appeal

As Johnson had hoped, the writers of the Harlem Renaissance were read not just by other African Americans, but by whites as well. By the end of the

1920s, African American writing had become part of mainstream literature. Even historically all-white communities could not help but notice black writers and their talents.

The authors of the Harlem Renaissance were pleased that so many whites were drawn to their work. They benefited financially from a wider readership, and they recognized that the number of white readers indicated that society's attitude toward blacks might be changing. Still, writing to please white people was not the goal. As Hughes wrote in an essay published in 1926, "We younger Negro artists who create now intend to express our individual dark-skinned selves without fear or shame. If white people are pleased we are glad. If they are not, it doesn't matter."[40] The greater purpose of the Harlem Renaissance, Hughes argued, was for writers to express the hardships, joys, and dreams of American blacks, and to do so in a way that was honest and true to life.

The diversity of the people who wrote during the Harlem Renaissance was perhaps the movement's most striking characteristic. At times, however, it was the movement's greatest weakness. The diversity of opinions and backgrounds often led to vocal disagreements. Author and critic Richard Wright disliked and criticized Hurston's novel *Their Eyes Were Watching God*, for example. Older authors counseled younger writers to avoid controversial topics, such as prostitution and alcoholism, and were angry when the younger writers ignored their advice. "*Home to Harlem* ... nauseates me," DuBois wrote about one of McKay's books, "and after the dirtier parts of its filth I feel distinctly like taking a bath."[41]

Then again, the movement's diversity was also its greatest strength. The Harlem Renaissance was defined not by art or by style, but by time, geography, and, most of all, race. The tie that bound these men and women together was not their writing, but themselves. Despite their bickering, the writers of the Harlem Renaissance generally saw themselves as part of a movement— and acted as such. They read each other's work, learned from one another, and built on their peers' achievements. They painted an increasingly full picture of what it was like to be black in America. They wrote to help create a brighter future for African Americans. "We build our temples for tomorrow, strong as we know how," Hughes wrote in a 1926 essay, "and we will stand on top of the mountain, free within ourselves."[42]

A MUSICAL RENAISSANCE

The Harlem Renaissance was mostly a movement of writers, but it included other art forms as well. That was particularly true of music. Star musicians—from blues singer Ethel Waters to jazz trumpeter and singer Louis Armstrong—performed concerts in venues such as the Apollo Theater in New York City. Ragtime pianist Eubie Blake, bandleader Duke Ellington, and vocalist Paul Robeson were all important parts of the Harlem musical world during the 1920s and 1930s.

No musical figure was more closely associated with Harlem than blues singer Bessie Smith. Smith grew up as part of a poor family in the rural South, but the quality of her voice and the emotions she expressed with it helped her become a famous entertainer. She was best known for performing classic blues songs, such as "Nobody Knows You When You're Down and Out" and "St. Louis Blues." She was renowned not just for her musical talent, but also for her wide range of emotional themes. To many African Americans, Smith's music represented their pain after more than a century of oppression.

Bessie Smith's beautiful voice and passionate performances of classic blues songs led to her fame as a singer.

The Harlem Renaissance repre-sented an impressive flowering of African American literature. Despite its success, the movement did not last long. The Great Depression, which began in 1929, forced dozens of pub-lishers out of business, limiting the market for black writers. As economic conditions worsened, Harlem became increasingly poor, its crime rates rose, and its status as the center of African American life and art was no longer secure. At the same time, the writers of the Harlem Renaissance began drifting apart, both personally and artistically. Some fought with each other, leaving rifts that never healed. A few stopped writing altogether. The rest no longer saw themselves as part of a movement. Historians debate when the Harlem Renaissance came to an end, but most agree that by 1939, the movement was over. The next great period of African American literature, however, was not long in coming.

CHAPTER FIVE

CIVIL RIGHTS STORIES: 1940–1969

The Harlem Renaissance brought black artists and writers together and gave national attention to their work. Entering the 1940s, African American literature started becoming more and more political, reflecting the push for equality that was taking hold across the country. The writers of this period drew inspiration from the authors of the past and from the contemporary events of the civil rights movement. This movement called for equality and civil rights for all people, regardless of the color of their skin, and it gained momentum throughout the 1950s and 1960s. The writers of the time joined their voices to these calls for justice.

Assimilation

Similar to the writers of the Harlem Renaissance, the African American authors of the 1940s and early 1950s were a diverse group. Many of them, however, did share a goal: wanting to assimilate. Their intent was to move into the mainstream and become known as American writers—not African American writers. Some critics have called this "raceless" writing. These men and women tried to avoid writing styles, language, or subject matter that could be seen as obviously African American. The aim of the black writer, one critic wrote in 1949, should be to become "an American writer ... as free as any [other American] to tap the rich literary resources of our land and its people."[43]

To be sure, some of this sentiment was present during the Harlem Renaissance as well. Langston Hughes emphasized his identity as an American; Countee Cullen and Claude McKay claimed traditional English poetry as part of their own

Frank Yerby was a black author who wrote historical novels about ancient times. He did not deal explicitly with racial issues in his writing.

heritage. In the years immediately following World War II, many black writers made a conscious effort to downplay race and racial issues in their writing. Among the most prominent of these was Georgia native Frank Yerby, a writer of historical novels about topics such as medieval Europe and classical Greece. For Yerby, this broad thematic focus was a recipe for success. In 1946, his novel *The Foxes of Harrow* reached best-seller lists, the first book by an African American author to do so.

Other writers of the period also worked with nonracial themes. Ann Petry grew up in a small Connecticut town populated mostly by whites. Though her first novel dealt with a poor black woman in Harlem, her second novel, published in 1947, was set in a New England town similar to the one where she grew up. It contained few African American characters and was not specifically concerned with those characters' struggles and dreams. In 1948, Zora Neale Hurston, remembered today for the strength of her black characters and her powerful interest in African American folklore, published a novel, *Seraph on the Suwanee*, that featured white characters.

Native Son

Even as many black writers were moving further into the mainstream during the 1940s, a few continued to focus on African Americans and their struggles against a white world. One of these authors was Richard Wright. Born in Mississippi in 1908, Wright was publishing stories and essays by the early 1930s. In 1940, Wright published a novel, *Native Son*, which is widely considered an American classic. It appears on many modern-day lists of the greatest English-language novels compiled by literary critics.

Growing up in Mississippi, Wright experienced a lot of racism, and he worked themes of racial prejudice into his writings. *Native Son*, for example, tells the story of Bigger Thomas, a young man from a poor urban neighborhood. Bigger is frequently in trouble with the law, which Wright attributes partly to Bigger's bad choices but also to the overwhelming discrimination of the time. In the book, Bigger responds to his lack of opportunities with anger, violence, and despair. To Wright, Bigger stood for African Americans everywhere. "No American Negro exists," he wrote, "who does not have his private Bigger Thomas living in his skull."[44]

Native Son, *Richard Wright's most famous novel, is still popular in the 21st century.*

Some critics and readers, including many whites, praised Wright's work for its realistic portrayal of African American life and its unflinching examination of racism. "Only a Negro could have written [it]," a reviewer for *TIME* magazine stated about *Native Son*, "but until now no Negro has possessed either the talent or the daring to write it."[45] Others, however, including some notable black writers, were highly critical of Wright's work. Their particular concern was Wright's heavy focus on race. In an essay directed largely at Wright and *Native Son*, for example, writer James Baldwin complained that by looking at Bigger solely as a black person, Wright made his main character an exaggeration instead of a fully developed human being.

The criticism coming from Baldwin and other writers did not change Wright's way of thinking. In 1945, Wright published an influential memoir, *Black Boy*. Like his controversial novel, *Black Boy* describes events clearly and realistically, making no attempt to hide the violence, poverty, and racism that Wright experienced throughout his life. In one section, for example, Wright describes working in a southern hotel where patrons and white staff members routinely bullied, threatened, and hit black employees. The laws and customs of the time forced the workers to put up with these behaviors—and to pretend that working at the hotel was a delight. "The maids, the hall-boys, and the bell-boys were all smiles," Wright explained. "They had to be."[46]

Tensions Between Writers

The black writers of the early 1950s drew from the themes of authors such as Wright, but they were also influenced by the raceless ideas of other African American writers. One of the best-known writers of this period was Baldwin. Though Baldwin disapproved of Wright's literary style, Baldwin's fiction was known for descriptions of urban blacks and African American life. His novel *Go Tell It on the Mountain*, published in 1952, is an excellent example. A semiautobiographical account of a black boy growing up in Harlem, the book drew readers into the details of African American family life and the world of the black church. Though the book was far from wholly positive about blacks and their lives, Baldwin was clear that he did not mean it to be a protest novel.

Another important writer of the period was a Chicago poet named Gwendolyn Brooks. Like Wright, Brooks did not shy away from racial issues—but she rarely made race and discrimination the center of her work. In a series of poems published in 1949, for example, Brooks described the life of Annie Allen, a young black woman. The poems are much more concerned with Allen's personal growth than with the unfairness of the world around her.

Perhaps the most famous writer of this era was Ralph Ellison. Born in 1914, Ellison is best known today for his 1952 novel, *Invisible Man*. This novel describes the life of a black man, never identified by name, who believes that he is metaphorically invisible—the people around him never really notice him or care to learn much about him. The novel shows the narrator moving from a small town to an all-black college and on to New York City, where he looks for work and becomes involved in political activity.

In some ways, *Invisible Man* reflects the themes of Wright's *Native Son* and *Black Boy*. Racism, for example, plays an obvious role in Ellison's novel. However, *Invisible Man* also describes how other blacks fail the narrator. The African American college president sabotages the narrator's job search; the narrator's black political allies have no interest in getting to know him as a person. The narrator's feelings of invisibility are partly due to his race—but in other ways, Ellison makes clear, these feelings are simply part of human life in general.

By the early 1950s, there were three important strands of African American literature: the raceless style, represented by writers such as Yerby; the deeply political style, represented by Wright; and the mix of the two, represented by authors such as Baldwin, Brooks, and Ellison. As Baldwin's essay attacking Wright's fondness for protest novels showed, the writers associated with each emerging style did not always coexist comfortably. Those tensions did not last long. Beginning in the late 1950s, as the civil rights movement really picked up nationwide, African American writers began to put aside their differences and come together as never before.

A Political Movement

In the late 1940s, tired of being mistreated, blacks across the South began to demand equal civil rights. Though the basic American rights, such as the right to vote, were technically granted to blacks by the 13th, 14th, and 15th Amendments, dozens of laws prevented African Americans from exercising those rights. By the early 1950s, the protesters had joined to form an organized movement. In the coming years, civil rights activists won many important victories. They convinced the U.S. Supreme Court to rule that segregation in school systems was against the law. They forced states to repeal laws that restricted the right of

Ralph Ellison was the author of Invisible Man, *which is one of the most famous and influential American novels of all time.*

blacks to vote. They eventually promoted the Civil Rights Act of 1964, which not only prohibited racial discrimination in public life, but also gave the federal government the power to penalize those who continued to discriminate. Few social movements in American history have accomplished so much.

The movement also met with significant opposition, however, especially from white southerners. Some school districts shut down altogether rather than allow blacks and whites to share classrooms, and angry whites reacted violently toward blacks in their communities. "Segregation now, segregation tomorrow and segregation forever,"[47] Alabama governor George Wallace promised his voters in 1963. Many state and local governments did everything they could to prevent blacks from voting, regardless of the new laws. Police forces in a number of communities brutally attacked civil rights protesters. Some civil rights leaders, among them Martin Luther King Jr., paid for their activism with their lives.

The civil rights movement brought black people of all backgrounds together and gave them a shared experience, a shared goal, and a shared identity. Interest in black folklore and black history boomed, and activists looked to the past for strength and encouragement. Protesters sang modified spirituals—based on the music of their enslaved ancestors—as they marched for their rights; speakers quoted Frederick Douglass, W.E.B. DuBois, and earlier black thinkers.

Black writers responded accordingly. Between the late 1950s and the end of the 1960s, black literature became openly and proudly about African Americans and their experience. Whether celebrating black history, publishing poems of protest, or writing novels about urban black life, the writers of the civil rights era focused on black culture and heritage and demanded rights for themselves and their people. More than ever before, African American writers were speaking with a single, unified voice.

Writing for Civil Rights

The civil rights movement had an impact on the way some veteran black writers thought about their work. Baldwin's *The Fire Next Time*, published in 1963, was one example. Though Baldwin had earlier complained about Richard Wright's aggressive perspective on race and race relations, *The Fire Next Time*

CIVIL RIGHTS LEADERS

Several leaders of the civil rights movement made invaluable contributions to African American literature. *Letter from a Birmingham Jail*, written by Martin Luther King Jr. after he was arrested during a 1963 protest march, describes many of King's core principles in clear, eloquent language. King's "I Have a Dream" speech, given at the Lincoln Memorial later in 1963, is among the most famous American speeches ever. In it, King described his vision for an America in which skin color and ethnic heritage do not matter. He envisioned an America in which all people would be able to enjoy the same rights and freedoms regardless of their heritage.

Malcolm X, another important leader, also added to the writings that sprang from the civil rights movement. More radical than King, Malcolm's message appealed particularly to poor urban black men with little education and less hope for a bright future. Malcolm's speeches and writings reflected his image of black America—an image often vastly different from King's vision. In particular, where King was always hopeful that peaceful integration would be a success, Malcolm was much less optimistic. Like the best of King's works, Malcolm's autobiography has long been acknowledged for its literary—as well as political—merit.

Martin Luther King Jr., one of the most famous civil rights leaders in history, wrote many powerful speeches that influenced the course of African American literature.

represented a shift in his thinking. This book was an honest discussion of race in America—and an attack on the whites who allowed discrimination to occur. "How can one respect, let alone adopt, the values of a people who do not, on any level whatever, live the way they say they do, or the way they say they should?"[48] Baldwin wrote.

Much of Brooks's poetry from this period also explicitly addressed civil rights themes. One of her most haunting works fictionalizes the 1955 death of Emmett Till, a 14-year-old boy murdered by an angry mob in Mississippi after he allegedly whistled at a white woman. Brooks wrote movingly of the "gradual dulling of those Negro eyes"[49] as he is killed. Themes such as these were common in Brooks's work during this time.

The writers who most clearly reflected the literary themes of the time, however, were new writers who came of age during the unstable years of protest. Among the most important of these was a poet and playwright named LeRoi Jones, born in New Jersey in 1934. Jones was heavily influenced early in his writing career by young white poets who experimented with poetic styles and forms, and he moved easily within both black and white circles. By 1960, he seemed poised for a long and rewarding life at the cutting edge of the literary world.

In the early 1960s, however, Jones had a change of heart. Disheartened by the difficulties faced by civil rights protesters, Jones rejected white society and culture and took on an identity that was passionately African American. He began wearing African clothing and changed his name to Imamu Amiri Baraka. Baraka's poetry became highly political, often aggressively so, and it urged blacks of all nations to band together. In his poem "SOS," he wrote,

> Calling black people
> Calling all black people, man
>   woman child
> Wherever you are, calling you,
>   urgent, come in
> Black People, come in, wherever
>   you are, urgent, calling[50]

By the mid-1960s, Baraka's writing had become a ferocious attack on the American system. His poems, plays, and prose attacked the United States, white Americans—whether they supported the civil rights movement or not—and blacks who Baraka believed were not radical enough. As Baraka wrote in an essay, the civil rights struggle was about making sweeping changes in the status of black people—and making these changes in any way necessary, even if that meant completely destroying contemporary American society.

Portrayals of Everyday Life

Many other black writers of the civil rights era followed Baraka's lead by producing deeply political works, though usually of a more subtle nature. Lorraine Hansberry's play *A Raisin in the Sun* is one example. It demonstrates the connection between politics and literature in this era. The play, dating from 1959, was the first drama written by an African American woman to be produced on Broadway. *A Raisin in the Sun* is about a black family's attempts in Chicago to navigate an often-hostile world. When the family buys a house in an all-white neighborhood, for example, their prospective neighbors try to keep them from moving in. *A Raisin in the Sun* has a positive ending—family members continue to pursue their dreams despite the obstacles—but prejudice is a centerpiece of the play.

Some African American writings of the period were less overtly political. Still, they echoed the political

A Raisin in the Sun *is a play that explores the experience of a black family living in a predominantly white community.*

AUTOBIOGRAPHIES AND *ROOTS*

Born in 1921 in Ithaca, New York, Alex Haley produced important works both during the civil rights era and afterward. In the early 1960s, while working as a journalist, Haley frequently interviewed civil rights leader Malcolm X. Before long, Haley and Malcolm decided to turn these interviews into a full-length book. Though the finished product was called *The Autobiography of Malcolm X*, it was a joint effort from the beginning, and Haley received full credit for his part in the work. The book was published in 1965, shortly after Malcolm was assassinated, and was a popular and critical success.

Haley is probably more famous today, however, for a book he published in 1976, more than 10 years after the publication of the *Autobiography*. This new book was called *Roots: The Saga of an American Family*. Partly fictionalized but largely based on fact, the book took the reader through generations of Haley's family history, beginning with an ancestor who was born in Africa and brought to North America as a slave. The following year, *Roots* was made into a wildly successful television miniseries. Together, the book and the miniseries sparked an enormous interest in genealogy and family history, particularly among African Americans.

Malcolm X, shown here, ranks alongside Martin Luther King Jr. as one of the most famous activists of the civil rights movement. Thanks in part to Alex Haley, his autobiography was published in 1965.

changes in America by celebrating black life and taking pride in their race. In 1969, poet Mari Evans wrote,

> I am a black woman
> tall as a cypress
> strong
> beyond all definition ...
> assailed
> impervious
> indestructible
> Look
> on me and be
> renewed[51]

Other writers explored African American history. As the new generation of writers saw it, African Americans of the 1960s needed to understand the history of their people in order to make their way in the world. The most accessible way to learn about black history was through the eyes of heroic figures—from Martin Luther King Jr. to ancient African folk characters.

Still other writers concentrated on describing the lives of ordinary black people. Although racial discrimination was present in most of these works, and black history often played a role as well, the emphasis in these works tended to be on individuals: their work, their play, and their families.

Ernest J. Gaines, for example, wrote about life in rural Louisiana in books such as *Bloodline* and *Of Love and Dust*, both published in the late 1960s. Paule Marshall, the Brooklyn-born daughter of parents from Barbados, described the lives of Caribbean immigrants in her novel *Brown Girl, Brownstones*. Books that focused on individuals and family life had been part of the Harlem Renaissance, but during the civil rights era, the number of novels on this theme vastly increased.

Similarities and Differences

In many ways, the writings of the civil rights movement are as different from one another as the works of the Harlem Renaissance. There is a large gap in tone between the uncompromising rhetoric of Baraka's essays, for example, and the much more subtle poetry of Brooks. Evans's proud declaration of blackness contrasts with the struggles of Marshall's Barbadian immigrants to come to terms with what it means to be black in a new land.

Even so, the works of the civil rights era show a remarkable consistency at heart. After a decade or two in which African American writers drifted in different directions, the civil rights movement unified them again. The political struggles of the time forced black writers to confront the reality that they were black in a society built and run largely by—and often for—whites. As a result, the writings of the civil rights era were openly political in a way that was not true of the colonial period, the Harlem Renaissance, or most other periods in African American literature. By reinforcing the message of the protest movement, the literature of the civil rights era ultimately helped to change the status of blacks in the American South.

The African American authors of the late 1950s and the 1960s addressed the same basic theme in their writing: what it was like to be black in a white world. Honest, unflinching, and deeply evocative of America during the civil rights years, the writing of the period is of historic importance—and of exceptional literary value.

CHAPTER SIX
TODAY'S STORIES: 1970–PRESENT

From the 1970s to today, African American literature has continued to grow in volume and influence. As African American literature has become more diverse, it has become harder to define. The earliest black writers mostly published nonfiction, while the writers of the Harlem Renaissance explored the experience of being black in their creative fiction. The civil rights movement predominantly featured political writing.

Today, black authors have broken into every genre of publishing—from poetry to political speeches and from romance novels to song lyrics. The influence of earlier writers is still prominent, and present-day authors such as Toni Morrison include images from folklore and the oral tradition in their novels. Many authors today still write about politics, and there are many new literary depictions of the experience of being black in America. The last several decades have been filled with an array of diverse contributions to African American literature.

I Know Why the Caged Bird Sings

There have been many important black writers over the past few decades. Of these men and women, though, one stands out for the length and breadth of her career and the enormous influence she has had on other writers: Maya Angelou. Through her dozens of published works, she has done as much as anyone to create and define the modern era of African American literature—and ranks as perhaps the most significant writer of the 20th century.

Born in St. Louis, Missouri,

Maya Angelou is known for her poetry and memoirs. She passed away in 2014.

in 1928, Angelou had a long and extremely varied career—not all of it focused on literature. As a young adult, she was active in the civil rights movement, for example. Angelou also worked as a college professor, as well as an actor, dancer, and film director. She is, however, best known for her writing, most notably her poetry. In 1993, she attracted national attention by reading her poem "On the Pulse of Morning" at the inauguration of President Bill Clinton, and she is one of America's best-selling poets.

Although poetry made Angelou famous, critics also admire her for a series of memoirs. The first of these books, *I Know Why the Caged Bird Sings*, follows Angelou from early childhood to high school graduation. Emotionally intense and written in a style more reminiscent of a novel than a standard autobiography, *I Know Why the Caged Bird Sings* was an immediate success upon its publication in 1969. Critics praised Angelou's use of language, her ability to evoke the rural South of her childhood, and her sensitive handling of difficult topics. "Maya Angelou writes like a song," one reviewer wrote, "and like the truth."[52]

The subject matter of *I Know Why the Caged Bird Sings* was instantly compelling. The book tells of Angelou's abandonment by both parents at an early age, describes the constant racism she experienced growing up in a small Arkansas town, and reveals that she was raped as a girl by her mother's boyfriend. Despite the dark and serious subject matter, though, the book also has many uplifting passages. At one point, for example, Angelou learns the power of spoken words when an adult reads to her from a novel. "I heard poetry for the first time in my life," Angelou wrote. "Her voice slid in and curved down through and over the words. She was nearly singing ... Her reading was a wonder in my ears."[53]

The success of *I Know Why the Caged Bird Sings* and the other memoirs that followed it encouraged other American writers to publish memoirs of their own. Many of these writers, moreover, were deeply influenced by the expressive artistry of Angelou's language and the novel-like narrative techniques she used in her works. So many subsequent memoirs were modeled after Angelou's that some critics argue that Angelou invented the modern American autobiography.

The Impact of Feminism

Angelou was also a pioneer for her

inclusion of feminist ideas in her work. Feminism is a social movement that first gained prominence in the 1970s as activists sought to improve the lives of women. Besides tearing down the barriers that kept women from achieving full equality with men, feminists also hoped to bring the experience of being female to the mainstream. Women's perspectives were too often ignored, feminists argued, and as a result, many women believed that their experiences did not matter. Just as blacks fought racial discrimination during the civil rights movements, feminists sought to reduce gender discrimination. To begin this fight, feminist leaders encouraged women to share the stories of their lives as women. Their goal was twofold: to help women reclaim their voices and to help them realize that their experiences were important.

In the beginning, feminism was primarily a movement of well-educated, upper–middle class white women. By the beginning of the 1970s, though, it was beginning to have a significant impact on black women as well. *I Know Why the Caged Bird Sings* was among the first books by an African American to express a feminist consciousness. Angelou's memoir is not simply about growing up black in America; rather, it is about growing up both black and female. Black women, Angelou wrote, are trapped in the "crossfire of masculine prejudice, white illogical hate and Black lack of power."[54]

The success of *I Know Why the Caged Bird Sings* helped turn conventional publishing wisdom upside down. For years, publishers had put their resources into selling books by male authors, such as Richard Wright and Ralph Ellison, and devoted less energy and money to women's writings. Angelou's work, however, proved as popular as anything written by a black man, and publishers took notice. *I Know Why the Caged Bird Sings* helped usher in an era of new opportunities for black female writers.

The Color Purple

Following in Angelou's footsteps, many writers since 1970 in African American literature have been extremely talented women. Among the most prominent of these is Alice Walker. Born in 1944, Walker grew up in Georgia when segregation was still in force. From very early on, she impressed people with her intelligence and curiosity. "She could outspell children twice her age," her first teacher recalled. "A lot of children passed my way, but Alice Walker was the smartest one I ever had."[55]

During and after college, Walker was active in both the women's rights and civil rights movements. Both movements influenced Walker's writing. The connections are easy to see in Walker's first novel, *The Third Life of Grange Copeland*, which was published in 1970. The main character, Grange Copeland, is a poor black farmer who is repeatedly mocked and harassed by a white man. Copeland deals with his frustrations by beating his wife. When Copeland's son grows up and marries, he treats his own wife the same way. "It was his rage at himself, and his life and his world that made him beat her," Walker wrote, describing the son. "His rage could and did blame *everything*, everything on her."[56] Walker's message was that the racial discrimination in America had far-reaching consequences.

Walker's best-known novel today is *The Color Purple*, which appeared in 1982 and was later made into a successful movie featuring Whoopi Goldberg and Oprah Winfrey. As a young teenager, the main character, Celie, is raped by her father, forced to give up two children, and beaten by her husband. At one point in the novel, she feels abandoned even by God. "The God I been praying and writing to is a man," she tells a friend. "And act just like all the other mens I know. Trifling, [forgetful], and lowdown."[57] However, things ultimately improve for Celie. She is finally able to stand up to her husband and make a new and more successful life for herself.

Toni Morrison

Toni Morrison, born in Lorain, Ohio, in 1931, was another female writer who helped make the experiences of African American women an important and essential part of black literature. The first African American author to be awarded the Nobel Prize in Literature in 1993, her influence is undeniable. Morrison published her first novel, *The Bluest Eye*, in 1970. Similar to the works of Walker and Angelou, *The Bluest Eye* focuses on the impact of racial issues on African American girls and women. The title of the novel comes from the desire of one of the characters, a black girl, to have blue eyes—a painful indication that she would prefer not to be African American.

ALICE WALKER

Alice Walker's novel *The Color Purple* has been widely praised for its realism, its vivid characters, and its emotional tale of a young woman who manages to overcome the tragedies of her life. One of the most enthusiastic assessments of the novel comes from Peter S. Prescott, a book critic who served as a judge on the panel that awarded *The Color Purple* the Pulitzer Prize for Fiction in 1983:

Over time, The Color Purple *has achieved a status few books ever attain. It is one of the few books that is read by most students in the country. It has become a rite of passage.*

It is also one of the few literary books to capture the popular imagination and leave a permanent imprint on our society. There are some commercial books that did that, like The Godfather ... *But* The Color Purple *is literature of the highest form.*[1]

1. Quoted in Mary Donnelly, *Alice Walker: The Color Purple and Other Works*. New York, NY: Marshall Cavendish Benchmark, 2010, p. 43.

The Bluest Eye was a success both commercially and critically. However, Morrison is best known today for two later novels: *Song of Solomon*, published in 1977, and 1988's *Beloved*. Both novels are based on themes from black history and folklore. *Song of Solomon* springs from a legend that a group of slaves once sprouted wings and flew back to Africa. *Beloved* is based on the true story of fugitive slave Margaret Garner. Both novels were extremely popular with critics as well as with the general public; *Beloved* won the Pulitzer Prize for Fiction, and in 2006, a group of critics voted it the best American novel since 1980. Both novels have also been widely praised for the beauty of the writing as well as for the significance of the messages the books contain. For Morrison, just like for many other African American authors, both the political and artistic aspects of her writing are equally important.

The success of Angelou, Walker,

Toni Morrison's novels use lyrical language to explore the devastating impact of racism on her characters.

and Morrison has had an obvious impact on other African American women writers. From folklorist and novelist Virginia Hamilton to poet Rita Dove, many black women have risen to prominence in the literary world in part because of the works of these three pioneering women. Additionally, Angelou, Walker, and Morrison have helped bring male African American writers to the public's attention. At no other point in African American history have books by black authors sold as well as they sell in modern times; at no other point have African American writers, male or female, received the critical acclaim that they do today.

Stories About Ordinary People

Many themes used by African American writers today reflect themes common in earlier eras of black literature. The lives of ordinary black people, the struggles of black immigrants—these and other themes appear frequently in the works of modern African American authors, just as they did in the works of the post–Civil War period or the Harlem Renaissance. One example is the work of playwright August Wilson. Born in Pittsburgh,

Pennsylvania, in 1945, Wilson is known today for a series of plays about black life in Pittsburgh during the 1900s. Two of these plays, *Fences* and *The Piano Lesson*, won the Pulitzer Prize for Drama. In 2016, *Fences* was adapted into a feature-length film that was highly regarded by both audiences and critics. Actress Viola Davis won both an Academy Award and a Golden Globe for her performance in the film. Like earlier writers, such as Langston Hughes and Lorraine Hansberry, Wilson was noted for his ability to write honestly about the lives of ordinary African Americans.

Still other writers followed the lead of authors such as Richard Wright, who had written unflinchingly of life among the poorest of African Americans. An author known as Sapphire published a novel titled *Push* in 1996. Though the subject matter was distressing—the novel dealt with themes such as illiteracy, incest, and abuse—the book sold extremely well. In 2009, the novel was made into a successful movie titled *Precious*.

Some authors have focused on the theme of immigration. From Phillis Wheatley to Claude McKay, many great black writers over the years have been immigrants. Among black immigrant writers today, Edwidge Danticat and Jamaica Kincaid stand out. Both of these women were born in the Caribbean and came to the United States as teenagers. Danticat's *Breath, Eyes, Memory*, published in 1994, and Kincaid's *Annie John*, which appeared in 1985, describe the challenges faced by newcomers to the United States.

Diverse Ways of Telling Stories

The modern era has seen remarkable growth in genre fiction—that is, fiction that fits into categories such as romance, science fiction, and mystery. For many years, black writers were not typically involved in these branches of publishing. Even today, most authors of genre fiction are white. Even so, the number of African Americans recognized for their contributions to these fields is growing steadily.

Octavia E. Butler, for example, is a noted science fiction and fantasy writer. Born in 1947 in California, Butler was drawn to science fiction as a girl. She has published a series of novels that deals with a unique being named Doro who is thousands of years old; these books have sold well among African Americans and among fans of science fiction in general. One of Butler's most familiar works is a time-travel novel titled *Kindred*, which was published in 1988. This book tells of a young black woman of the present day who suddenly finds herself on a southern plantation before the Civil War.

Several African American writers have published successful mystery novels. The most famous of these writers is Walter Mosley. Born in Michigan in 1952, Mosley has written a number of books about a private detective named Easy Rawlins. Rawlins, a veteran of World War II, solves crimes in Los Angeles. Though some critics look down on mystery fiction and other genre books as not being sophisticated, Mosley has defended his work. Different genres allow authors, especially African Americans, to explore complex topics that do not fall into the categories of nonfiction or historical fiction.

The modern era in African American literature also includes a new focus on the combination of writing with other art forms. One of the most important of these writers is Ntozake Shange, born

STORIES FOR YOUNG PEOPLE

As is true of mysteries, romance novels, and other types of genre fiction, the market for young adult books has boomed since the 1980s. Virginia Hamilton, a writer from Ohio, was one of the first black novelists to earn success in this field. Before her death in 2002, Hamilton published several well-received books of folklore, including *The People Could Fly* and *Her Stories*, aimed primarily at young people. She is also known for her young adult fiction, notably her novels *Zeely* and *The House of Dies Drear*, along with *M.C. Higgins, the Great*, which won the Newbery Medal as the best children's novel of 1975. Though Hamilton's folklore looks to the past, her novels are most often set in contemporary times.

Mildred D. Taylor is another modern author who is best known for her writing for young people. Her work focuses on African American history; her novels *Roll of Thunder, Hear My Cry*, and *Let the Circle Be Unbroken* each describe what life was like for blacks in the South during the years before the civil rights movement. Both of these novels won awards and remain widely read today. Taylor has also written books set in the pre–Civil War South.

Two African American men have also written extensively for young adults. One, Walter Dean Myers, writes most often of children growing up in Harlem during the present day. His novels deal with controversial topics such as drug abuse and gang violence. One of his best-known works to date is *Scorpions*, which was nominated for a Newbery Medal in 1989. Christopher Paul Curtis has won awards for historical novels such as *Bud, Not Buddy*—set in Michigan during the 1930s—and *The Watsons Go to Birmingham–1963*, which deals with a northern black family's arrival in Alabama at a critical point in the civil rights movement.

in New Jersey in 1948. Several of Shange's works combine poetry, music, and dance into one dramatic composition. Performers dance and recite the words to poems on a stage without sets, props, or backdrops. Shange is best known today for a work titled *For Colored Girls Who Have Considered Suicide / When the Rainbow Is Enuf*. The work is meant to be performed by seven women, each dressed in a different color.

Other black writers of the modern age are likewise concerned with more than just words. Gil

Scott-Heron, born in Chicago in 1949, is best remembered today for his poem "The Revolution Will Not Be Televised," which he often performed to the rhythm of drumbeats—a style that shares roots with rap and hip-hop music. This poem contains references to contemporary politicians and celebrities, along with advertising slogans and commercial products. Scott-Heron's meaning was that television and other forms of entertainment were distractions for black people that focused their attention away from the inequalities in the United States.

From Past to Present

From the rich oral tradition and folklore first brought by Africans to the Americas, to the contemporary literary and genre fiction by black authors, African American literature has grown and changed substantially throughout the years. Authors have explored new styles and themes in poetry, autobiographies, literary novels, song lyrics, and countless other genres. The work of African American authors has gone from being questioned and sidelined to taking a well-deserved spot on the broad shelf of American literature as a whole.

One of the best examples of the continued advancement of African Americans in the United States is Barack Obama. Not only did he break dozens of political boundaries for blacks—including serving as the first black president—he also achieved fame for his writing. In 1995, he released *Dreams from My Father: A Story of Race and Inheritance*, which was an inspirational memoir about both his father and himself. In 2006, his fame grew exponentially with the release of *The Audacity of Hope: Thoughts on Reclaiming the American Dream*. Some have argued that his international recognition after that book's release helped him win the presidency in 2008.

Today, African American authors such as Toni Morrison have won major literary prizes and awards; this is a far cry from being put on trial to determine whether a black woman could truly have written great poetry. Although much has changed, there are themes that have persevered throughout the ages to still show up in the work of today's black literary stars.

African American literature has affected and been affected by the political and historical struggle of black Americans to achieve equal rights and opportunities. The slave narratives of the past were of great importance to the abolitionist

MUSICAL EXPANSION

Literary critics once looked down on song lyrics, which they saw as something less than "true" literature. Today, however, that disapproval is much less widespread: Song lyrics are increasingly viewed as a form of poetry and a distinct literary genre, studied in university courses, and analyzed by scholars. Modern African American writers, accordingly, have made names for themselves as lyricists.

Some of the most famous of these songwriters work in the field of rap music. Kanye West is admired not only as a performer, but also as an excellent writer of rap lyrics. Other rap lyricists of note include Frank Ocean, Kendrick Lamar, and Drake, whose lyrics often have a romantic quality.

Still other African Americans are achieving success by writing lyrics in other genres. Mary J. Blige and will.i.am, for example, have written pop and R&B lyrics to great critical acclaim. Alice Randall, a novelist and professor who was born in 1959, has written the lyrics for many successful country songs; she collaborated with another writer to produce the 1994 hit "XXX's" and OOO's," which reached the top of the country music chart for singer Trisha Yearwood. Singer CeCe Winans is one of dozens of African American artists who have written popular gospel songs.

movement. Memoirs and autobiographies that explore what it means to be black in America have always played a crucial role in building empathy and respect from different groups. The fellowship built up by the authors involved in the Harlem Renaissance helped to connect black authors and build pride in their identity as African Americans as well as writers. Today, artists—ranging from singer Beyoncé to author and journalist Ta-Nehisi Coates—are still boldly discussing society and politics by using their public platform to voice their support for Black Lives Matter and other activist movements.

To this day, African American writers draw inspiration from those who came before them. Authors such as Toni Morrison and Zora Neale Hurston, along with many others, often include references to old African folktales in their work. The spirituals of the past are often quoted in the novels of the present—from the title of James Baldwin's novel

Go Tell It on the Mountain to the closing lines of Martin Luther King's "I Have a Dream" speech. It is safe to say that the literature being written today will then have a noticeable effect on the authors of tomorrow.

Despite resistance, lack of recognition, and outright exclusion from the broader literary stage, African American authors have refused to be silenced. They kept ancient stories alive by passing them down through generations, despite slavery's attempts to crush them. They confronted white publishers in Harlem with literary talent and broke through publishing barriers to get their words in front of larger audiences. Today, black authors challenge publishers and prize committees to diversify and expand their catalogues to include a variety of African American voices. They know that their stories and voices are important and must be heard, and those authors who have committed their stories and voices to the page—despite the obstacles standing in their way—will be heard for many years to come.

NOTES

Chapter One: Stories Spoken and Sung: 1600–1800

1. Roger D. Abrahams, *African American Folktales: Stories from Black Traditions in the New World*. New York, NY: Pantheon, 1985, p. 4.

2. Joel Chandler Harris, *The Complete Tales of Uncle Remus*. Boston, MA: Houghton Mifflin, 1983, p. 12.

3. Quoted in William Francis Allen, Charles Pickard Ware, and Lucy McKim Garrison, *Slave Songs of the United States*. Bedford, MA: Applewood, 1867, p. 88.

4. Quoted in Bruce Jackson, ed., *The Negro and His Folklore in Nineteenth-Century Periodicals*. Austin, TX: University of Texas Press, 1967, p. 94.

5. "When Israel Was in Egypt's Land," LutheranHymnal.com, accessed May 2, 2017. www.lutheran-hymnal.com/lyrics/hs825.htm.

6. Quoted in Mark A. Noll, *In the Beginning Was the Word: The Bible in American Public Life, 1492–1783*. Oxford, UK: Oxford University Press, 2016, p. 213.

7. Quoted in Faith Berry, *From Bondage to Liberation*. New York, NY: Continuum, 1996, p. 56.

8. Quoted in Faith Berry, *From Bondage to Liberation*, p. 55.

9. Quoted in John Wesley Cromwell, *The Negro in American History: Men and Women Eminent in the Evolution of the American of African Descent*. Washington, DC: The American Negro Academy, 1914, p. 84.

10. Quoted in Frances Smith Foster, "Resisting Incidents," in *Harriet Jacobs and Incidents in the Life of a Slave Girl: New Critical Essays*, Deborah M. Garfield and Rafia Zafar, eds. Cambridge, UK: Cambridge University Press, 1996, p. 59.

11. Phillis Wheatley, "On Being Brought from Africa to America," Poetry Foundation, accessed May 18, 2017. www.poetryfoundation.org/poems-and-poets/poems/detail/45465.

12. Lucy Terry Prince, "Bars Fight," PBS, accessed May 18, 2017. www.pbs.org/wgbh/aia/part2/2h1592t.html.

13. Arna Bontemps, ed., *Great Slave Narratives*. Boston, MA: Beacon, 1969, p. xii.

Chapter Two: Stories of Slavery: 1800–1865

14. David Walker, *Walker's Appeal, in Four Articles; Together with a Preamble, to the Coloured Citizens of the World, but in Particular, and Very Expressly, to Those of the United States of America, Written in Boston, State of Massachusetts, September 28, 1829*. Boston, MA: David Walker, 1830. HTML e-book, accessed May 18, 2017. docsouth.unc.edu/nc/walker/walker.html.

15. Walker, *Walker's Appeal*.

16. Henry Highland Garnet, "An Address to the Slaves of the United States of America," PBS, accessed May 18, 2017. www.pbs.org/wgbh/aia/part4/4h2937t.html.

17. Frances Ellen Watkins Harper, "The Slave Mother," Poetry Foundation, accessed May 18, 2017. www.poetryfoundation.org/poems-and-poets/poems/detail/51977.

18. Martin Robison Delany, "A Project for an Expedition of Adventure, to the Eastern Coast of Africa," in *Apropos of Africa: Sentiments of American Negro Leaders on Africa from the 1800s to the 1950s*, Adelaide Cromwell Hill and Martin Kilson, eds. London, UK: Frank Cass & Co., 1969, p. 22.

19. Moses Roper, *A Narrative of the Adventures and Escape of Moses Roper, from American Slavery*. Philadelphia, PA: Merrihew & Gunn, 1838. HTML e-book, accessed May 18, 2017. docsouth.unc.edu/fpn/roper/roper.html.

20. James W. C. Pennington, *The Fugitive Blacksmith*, in Yuval Taylor, ed., *I Was Born a Slave: An Anthology of Classic Slave Narratives*, vol. 2. Chicago, IL: Lawrence Hill, 1999, p. 121.

21. Olaudah Equiana, *The Interesting Narrative of the Life of Olaudah Equiano, or Gustavus Vassa, the African. Written by Himself*, vol. 2. London, UK: G. Vassa, 1789. HTML e-book, accessed May 18, 2017. docsouth.unc.edu/neh/equiano2/equiano2.html.

22. Henry Brown, *Narrative of Henry Box Brown, Who Escaped from Slavery Enclosed in a Box 3 Feet Long and 2 Wide. Written from a Statement of Facts Made by Himself. With Remarks Upon the Remedy for Slavery by Charles Stearns*, in *Understanding 19th-Century Slave Narratives*. Sterling Lecater Bland Jr., ed. Santa Barbara, CA: ABC-CLIO, 2016, p. 155.

23. Frederick Douglass, *Life of an American Slave*. Boston, MA: Anti-Slavery Office, 1845. HTML e-book, accessed May 18, 2017. utc.iath.virginia.edu/abolitn/abaufda14t.html.

24. Frederick Douglass, "The Meaning of July Fourth for the Negro," PBS, accessed May 18, 2017. www.pbs.org/wgbh/aia/part4/4h2927t.html.

Chapter Three: Postbellum Stories: 1865–1918

25. Paul Laurence Dunbar, "We Wear the Mask," Poetry Foundation. www.poetryfoundation.org/poems-and-poets/poems/detail/44203.

26. Booker T. Washington, "An Address Delivered at the Opening of the Cotton States and International Exposition," Library of Congress, accessed May 18, 2017. memory.loc.gov/ammem/aap/aapaddr.html.

27. Booker T. Washington, *Up from Slavery*. New York, NY: Signet Classics, 2010. PDF e-book.

28. W. E. B. DuBois, "The Souls of Black Folk," in *Classics of American Political and Constitutional Thought: Reconstruction to the Present*, Scott J. Hammond, Kevin R. Hardwick, and Howard Leslie Lubert, eds. Indianapolis, IN: Hackett Publishing, 2007, p. 196.

29. W. E. B. DuBois, "Of Our Spiritual Strivings," in *The Souls of Black Folk*. Chicago, IL: A. C. McClurg & Co., 1904, p. 3.

Chapter Four: New York City Stories: 1918–1940

30. James Weldon Johnson, "The Making of Harlem," in *Survey Graphic*, March 1925, p. 635.

31. Quoted in Christopher Buck, *Alain Locke: Faith and Philosophy*. Los Angeles, CA: Kalimát Press, 2005, p. 116.

32. Countee Cullen, "Yet Do I Marvel," Favorite Poem Project, accessed May 18, 2017. www.favoritepoem.org/poem_YetDoIMarvel.html.

33. Langston Hughes, "The Negro Speaks of Rivers," Academy of American Poets, accessed May 18, 2017. www.poets.org/poetsorg/poem/negro-speaks-rivers.

34. Zora Neale Hurston. *Their Eyes Were Watching God*. Urbana, IL: University of Illinois Press, 1937, p. 47.

35. Langston Hughes, "Cora Unashamed," in *The Short Stories of Langston Hughes*, Akida Sullivan Harper, ed. New York, NY: Hill and Wang, 1996, p. 41.

36. Langston Hughes, "I, Too," Poetry Foundation, accessed May 18, 2017. www.poetryfoundation.org/poems-and-poets/poems/detail/47558.

37. Nella Larsen, *Passing*. Mineola, NY: Dover Publications, 2004, p. 56.

38. Zora Neale Hurston, *The Complete Stories*. New York, NY: HarperPerennial, 1995, p. 25.

39. Quoted in Jon Michael Spencer, *Re-searching Black Music*. Knoxville, TN: University of Tennessee Press, 1996, p. 92.

40. Langston Hughes, "The Negro Artist and the Racial Mountain," Modern American Poetry, accessed May 18, 2017. www.english.illinois.edu/maps/poets/g_l/hughes/mountain.htm.

41. Quoted in Cromwell, *Apropos of Africa*, p. 297.

42. Langston Hughes, "The Negro Artist and the Racial Mountain."

Chapter Five: Civil Rights Stories: 1940–1969

43. Quoted in Yomna Mohamed Saber, *Brave to Be Involved: Shifting Positions in the Poetry of Gwendolyn Brooks*. Berlin, Germany: Peter Lang, 2010, p. 76.

44. Quoted in George M. Shulman, *American Prophecy: Race and Redemption in American Political Culture*. Minneapolis, MN: University of Minnesota Press, 2008, p. 153.

45. Quoted in Bill V. Mullen, *Popular Fronts: Chicago and African-American Cultural Politics, 1935–46*. Urbana, IL: University of Illinois Press, 1999, p. 31.

46. Richard Wright, "The Ethics of Living Jim Crow: An Autobiographical Sketch," American Stuff, accessed May 18, 2017. newdeal.feri.org/fwp/fwp03.htm.

47. Quoted in "'Segregation Forever': A Fiery Pledge Forgiven, but Not Forgotten," NPR, accessed May 18, 2017. www.npr.org/2013/01/14/169080969/segregation-forever-a-fiery-pledge-forgiven-but-not-forgotten.

48. James Baldwin, "Letter from a Region in My Mind," in *The 60s: The Story of a Decade*, Henry Finder, ed. New York, NY: Random House, 2016, pp. 27–28.

49. Gwendolyn Brooks, "A Bronzeville Mother Loiters in Mississippi. Meanwhile, a Mississippi Mother Burns Bacon," in *The Lynching of Emmett Till: A Documentary Narrative*, Christopher Metress, ed. Charlottesville, VA: University of Virginia Press, 2002, p. 315.

50. Quoted in Jay R. Berry, "Poetic Style in Amiri Baraka's Black Art," *CLA Journal*, December, 1988.

51. Mari Evans, "I Am a Black Woman," AfroPoets Famous Writers, accessed May 18, 2017. www.afropoets.net/marievans2.html.

Chapter Six: Today's Stories: 1970–Present

52. Quoted in Francesca Biller, "How Maya Angelou 'Frees' Us All from 'Our' Cages & Helps Us All to Sing," *Elephant*, May 28, 2014. www.elephantjournal.com/2014/05/how-maya-angelou-frees-us-all-from-our-cages-helps-us-all-to-sing.

53. Maya Angelou. *I Know Why the Caged Bird Sings*, in *The Collected Autobiographies of Maya Angelou*. New York, NY: Modern Library, 2004, pp. 79–80.

54. Quoted in Valérie Baisnée, *Gendered Resistance: The Autobiographies of Simone de Beauvoir, Maya Angelou, Janet Frame and Marguerite Duras*. Amsterdam, Netherlands: Rodopi, 1997, p. 74.

55. Quoted in Evelyn C. White. *Alice Walker: A Life*. New York, NY: Norton, 2004, p. 15.

56. Quoted in White, *Alice Walker*, p. 186.

57. Quoted in Francis L. Gross Jr., *Searching for God*. Kansas City, KS: Sheed & Ward, 1990, p. 122.

FOR MORE INFORMATION

Books

Angelou, Maya. *I Know Why the Caged Bird Sings*. New York, NY: Random House, 1969. This is a groundbreaking autobiographical account of growing up in the rural South during segregation and one of the first African American books to show the influence of the feminist movement.

Bragg, Beauty. *Reading Contemporary African American Literature: Black Women's Popular Fiction, Post-Civil Rights Experience, and the African American Canon*. Lanham, MD: Lexington Books, 2015. This book allows readers to access a deeper level of understanding of African American literature by outlining some of the most important genres in modern black writing.

Harris, Trudier. *Martin Luther King Jr., Heroism, and African American Literature*. Tuscaloosa, AL: University of Alabama Press, 2014. This detailed study discusses how modern African American authors have been influenced by one of black America's greatest heroes: Martin Luther King Jr.

Mance, Ajuan Maria. *Before Harlem: An Anthology of African American Literature from the Long Nineteenth Century*. Knoxville, TN: University of Tennessee Press, 2016. This vast anthology of black writings from colonial times to the start of the 20th century includes extensive notes on the writers and suggestions for further research.

Mathes, Christian. *Imagine the Sound: Experimental African American Literature After Civil Rights*. Minneapolis, MN: University of Minnesota Press, 2015.
This book offers a look at unique subgenres of black literature, focusing on authors who broke the conventional "rules" of writing.

Websites

Academy of American Poets (www.poets.org/index. php)
The Academy of American Poets runs this site, which has links to poems and biographies of influential poets throughout history, including many African Americans.

Digital Schomburg African American Women Writers of the 19th Century (digital.nypl.org/schomburg/writers_aa19/toc. html)
Hosted by the New York Public Library, this site exhibits poetry, fiction, and other works written by black women in the 1800s.

Slave Narratives and Uncle Tom's Cabin (www.pbs.org/wgbh/aia/ part4/4p2958.html)
PBS hosts a series detailing the lives of Africans in America, and this site has information on slave narratives, with links to further information related to African American literature.

"10 African-American Authors Everyone Should Read" (www.forbes.com/ sites/jamesmarshallc rotty/2012/02/18/10-african-american-authors-everyone-should-read/#4be838da2d14)
This well-researched article published by *Forbes* describes some of the most influential and important black writers throughout history.

Three Speeches from Frederick Douglass: Examples of His Passion, Logic and Power (www.frederickdouglass. org/speeches/index.html)
This site has the complete texts of three of Douglass's most famous speeches; the website links to a biography of Douglass and other information as well.

INDEX

A

American and Other Poems
(Whitfield), 36
Angelou, Maya, 7, 50, 85–90, 92
Annie John (Kincaid), 93
Armstrong, Louis, 68
Audacity of Hope, The (Obama), 95
Autobiography of Malcolm X, The
(Haley and Malcolm X), 82

B

Baldwin, James, 74–75, 77, 79, 97
Banneker, Benjamin, 12–13
Baraka, Imamu Amiri, 79–80, 83
"Bars Fight" (Prince), 22
Beloved (Morrison), 90
Between the World and Me (Coates), 7
Black Boy (Wright), 74–75
Black Lives Matter, 96
Blake, Eubie, 68
Blige, Mary J., 96
Bloodline (Gaines), 83
Bluest Eye, The (Morrison), 89
Bontemps, Arna, 23
Breath, Eyes, Memory (Danticat), 93
Br'er Rabbit tales, 13–15, 23, 45
Brooks, Gwendolyn, 75, 79, 83
Brown Girl, Brownstones (Marshall), 83
Brown, Henry, 37
Bud, Not Buddy (Curtis), 94
Butler, Octavia, 7, 93

C

Cane (Toomer), 59
Chesnutt, Charles W., 43–47, 53
Civil Rights Act (1964), 76–77
civil rights movement, 9, 70, 75,
77–79, 82–85, 87–89, 94
Clinton, Bill, 87
Coates, Ta-Nehisi, 7, 96
Color Purple, The (Walker), 88–90
Conjure Woman, The (Chesnutt), 44,
53
Craft, Ellen, 37
Craft, William, 37
Cullen, Countee, 60–63, 70
Curtis, Christopher Paul, 94

D

Danticat, Edwidge, 93
Delany, Martin, 28–30, 39
Douglass, Frederick, 6, 37–42, 77
Drake, 96
Dreams From My Father (Obama), 95
"Drenched in Light" (Hurston), 66
DuBois, W.E.B., 51–54, 58, 67, 77
Dunbar, Paul Laurence, 46–47, 53

E

Ellington, Duke, 68
Ellison, Ralph, 75–76, 88
Equiano, Olaudah, 31–34, 40–42
Evans, Mari, 83

"An Evening Thought. Salvation
  by Christ with Penitential Cries"
  (Hammon), 17
Exodus, 16–17

F
Father of the Blues (Handy), 45
Fauset, Jessie, 58, 60, 63–64
feminism, 87–88
Fences (Wilson), 92
Fire Next Time, The (Baldwin), 77
*For Colored Girls Who Have
  Considered Suicide / When the
  Rainbow is Enuf* (Shange), 94
Foxes of Harrow, The (Yerby), 72

G
Gaines, Ernest J., 83
Garner, Margaret, 90
Garnet, Henry Highland, 26, 41
Go Tell It on the Mountain (Baldwin),
  74, 97
Great Depression, 69

H
Haley, Alex, 82
Hamilton, Virginia, 92
Hammon, Jupiter, 17–19, 22–23, 55
Handy, W.C., 45
Hansberry, Lorraine, 80, 92
Harlem Renaissance, 9, 56, 58–70,
  83–85, 92, 96
Harper, Frances Ellen Watkins,
  26–28, 41–42
Harris, Joel Chandler, 13

Hidden Figures, 7
Home to Harlem (McKay), 67
House of Dies Drear, The
  (Hamilton), 94
Hughes, Langston, 6, 60–67, 70, 92
Hurston, Zora Neale, 60–61, 63–64,
  66–67, 72, 96

I
I Know Why the Caged Bird Sings
  (Angelou), 7, 50, 87–88
Incidents in the Life of a Slave Girl
  (Jacobs), 40
*Interesting Narrative of the Life
  of Olaudah Equiano or Gustavus
  Vassa, the African The* (Equiano),
  32–33
Invisible Man (Ellison), 75–76

J
Jacobs, Harriet, 40
Johnson, Charles S., 6, 58, 60, 66
Johnson, James Weldon, 46–48, 50,
  57
John tales, 15
Jones, LeRoi. *See* Baraka, Imamu
  Amiri

K
Kincaid, Jamaica, 93
Kindred (Butler), 93
King, Martin Luther, Jr., 77–78,
  82–83

L

Lamar, Kendrick, 96

Larsen, Nella, 62, 64, 66

Letter from a Birmingham Jail (King), 78

Let the Circle Be Unbroken (Taylor), 94

Lindsay, Vachel, 64

Locke, Alain, 60

M

Malcolm X, 78, 82

Marshall, Paule, 83

M.C. Higgins, the Great (Hamilton), 94

McKay, Claude, 62–65, 67, 70, 92

Morrison, Toni, 7, 85, 89–92, 95–96

Mosley, Walter, 93

Myers, Walter Dean, 94

N

Narrative of the Life of Frederick Douglass, an American Slave (Douglass), 6, 32, 37

National Urban League, 58

Native Son (Wright), 73–75

Nobel Prize, 7, 89

O

Obama, Barack, 95

Of Love and Dust (Gaines), 83

"On the Pulse of Morning" (Angelou), 87

Opportunity: Journal of Negro Life (magazine), 6, 58

oral tradition, 8, 11, 15–17, 22–23, 85, 95

P

Passing (Larsen), 66

Pennington, James, 31

People Could Fly, The (Hamilton), 94

Petry, Ann, 72

Piano Lesson, The (Wilson), 92

Precious (film), 92

Prescott, Peter S., 90

Prince, Lucy Terry, 22–23

Pulitzer Prize, 7, 90, 92

Push (Sapphire), 92

R

"raceless" writing, 70

Raisin in the Sun, A (Hansberry), 80–81

Randall, Alice, 96

"The Revolution Will Not Be Televised" (Scott-Heron), 95

Robeson, Paul, 68

Roll of Thunder, Hear My Cry (Taylor), 94

Roots: The Saga of an American Family (Haley), 82

Roper, Moses, 28–29, 31

Running a Thousand Miles for Freedom (Craft and Craft), 37

S

Sapphire, 92

science fiction, 7, 93

Scorpions (Myers), 94

Scott-Heron, Gil, 94–95

segregation, 42, 51, 76–77, 88

Seraph on the Suwanee (Hurston), 72

Shange, Ntozake, 93–94

slave narratives, 6, 28–31, 34–35, 37,
    39–40, 95–96

"The Slave Mother" (Harper), 28

Smith, Bessie, 68

Son of Solomon (Morrison), 90

Souls of Black Folk, The (DuBois),
    53–54

T

Taylor, Mildred, 94

Their Eyes Were Watching God
    (Hurston), 64, 67

Third Life of Grange Copeland, The
    (Walker), 89

Till, Emmett, 79

Toomer, Jean, 59

Tuskegee Normal and Industrial
    Institute, 49, 51–52

U

Underground Railroad, The
    (Whitehead), 7

Up from Slavery (Booker T.
    Washington), 49, 52–53

U.S. Supreme Court, 76

V

Van Doren, Carl, 58, 60

Vassa, Gustavus. *See* Equiano,
    Olaudah

W

Walker, Alice, 88–90, 92

Walker, David, 24–26, 28, 39, 41–42

Wallace, George, 77

Washington, Booker T., 49, 51–53

Washington, George, 12, 21

Waters, Ethel, 68

*Watsons Go to Birmingham—1963,
    The* (Curtis), 94

"We Wear the Mask" (Dunbar), 46

Wheatley, Phillis, 6, 19–22, 42, 53, 92

Whitehead, Colson, 7

Whitfield, James M., 36

will.i.am, 96

Wilson, August, 92

Winans, CeCe, 96

Wright, Richard, 67, 72–75, 77–78,
    88, 92

Y

Yerby, Frank, 71–72, 75

Z

Zeely (Hamilton), 94

PICTURE CREDITS

ABOUT THE AUTHOR

Meghan Sharif is a writer and avid reader. When her nose is not in a book, she works as a full-time teacher for adults with disabilities. In her free time, she enjoys yoga, crocheting, and kickboxing. She lives in Central Pennsylvania.